SO-BMS-197

Authority in language

The Authors

James Milroy is Professor of Linguistics at the University of Sheffield. He has also taught at the Universities of Colorado, Leeds, Manchester and Belfast. His previous books include *The Language of Gerard Manley Hopkins* (André Deutsch, 1977) and *Regional Accents of English: Belfast* (Blackstaff Press, 1981).

Lesley Milroy is Senior Lecturer in Speech at the University of Newcastle upon Tyne. She was previously Principal Lecturer in Linguistics at Ulster Polytechnic and Senior Simon Research Fellow at the University of Manchester. She is the author of *Language and Social Networks* (Blackwell, 1980).

Language, Education and Society

General Editor
Michael Stubbs
Department of Linguistics
University of Nottingham

Authority
in language

Investigating language
prescription and standardisation

James Milroy and *Lesley Milroy*

Routledge & Kegan Paul
London and New York

First published in 1985
by Routledge & Kegan Paul Ltd
11 New Fetter Lane, London EC4P 4EE

Published in the USA by
Routledge & Kegan Paul Inc.
in association with Methuen Inc.
29 West 35th Street, New York, NY 10001

First published as a paperback 1987

Set in Times 10 on 12 point
and printed in Great Britain
by Butler & Tanner

© *James Milroy and Lesley Milroy 1985*

No part of this book may be reproduced in
any form without permission from the publisher,
except for the quotation of brief passages
in criticism

Library of Congress Cataloging in Publication Data

Milroy, James.
Authority in language.

(Language, education, and society)
Bibliography: p.
Includes index.
1. Standard language.   2. English language—
Standardization.   3. Language and languages—Variation.
4. Communicative competence.   5. Language and languages—
Ability testing.   I. Milroy, Lesley.   II. Title.
III. Series.
P368.M54   1985   410   85–1847

ISBN 0–7100–9761–1 (c)
ISBN 0–7102–1201–1 (p)

Contents

General Editor's preface

Simply a list of some of the questions implied by the phrase *Language, Education and Society* gives an immediate idea of the complexity, and also the fascination, of the area.

How is language related to learning? Or to intelligence? How should a teacher react to Non-Standard dialect in the classroom? Do regional and social accents and dialects matter? What is meant by Standard English? Does it make sense to talk of 'declining standards' in language or in education? Or to talk of some children's language as 'restricted'? Do immigrant children require special language provision? How can their native languages be used as a valuable resource in schools? Can 'literacy' be equated with 'education'? Why are there so many adult illiterates in Britain and the USA? What effect has growing up with no easy access to language: for example, because a child is profoundly deaf? Why is there so much prejudice against people whose language background is odd in some way: because they are handicapped, or speak a non-standard dialect or foreign language? Why do linguistic differences lead to political violence, in Belgium, India, Wales and other parts of the world?

These are all real questions, of the kind which worry parents, teachers and policy-makers, and the answer to them is complex and not at all obvious. It is such questions that authors in this series discuss.

Language plays a central part in education. This is probably generally agreed, but there is considerable debate and confusion about the exact relationship between language and learning. Even though the importance of language is generally recognised, we still have a lot to learn about how language is related to either educational success or to intelligence and thinking. Language is also a central fact in everyone's social life. People's attitudes and most deeply held beliefs are at stake, for it is through language that personal and social identities are maintained and recognised. People are judged, whether justly or not, by the language they speak.

Language, Education and Society is therefore an area where scholars have a responsibility to write clearly and persuasively, in order to communicate the best in recent research to as wide an audience as possible. This means not only other researchers, but also all those who are involved in educational, social and political policy-making, from individual teachers to government. It is an area where value judgments cannot be avoided. Any action that we take – or, of course, avoidance of action – has moral, social and political consequences. It is vital, therefore, that practice is informed by the best knowledge available, and that decisions affecting the futures of individual children or whole social groups are not taken merely on the basis of the all too widespread folk myths about language in society.

Linguistics, psychology and sociology are often rejected by non-specialists as jargon-ridden; or regarded as fascinating, but of no relevance to educational or social practice. But this is superficial and short-sighted: we are dealing with complex issues, which require an understanding of the general principles involved. It is bad theory to make statements about language in use which cannot be related to educational and social reality. But it is equally unsound to base beliefs and action on anecdote, received myths and unsystematic or idiosyncratic observations.

All knowledge is value-laden: it suggests action and changes our beliefs. Change is difficult and slow, but possible nevertheless. When language in education and society is seriously and systematically studied, it becomes clear how awesomely complex is the linguistic and social knowledge of all children and adults. And with such an understanding, it becomes impossible to maintain a position of linguistic prejudice and intolerance. This may be the most important implication of a serious study of language, in our linguistically diverse modern world.

This book, *Authority in Language*, is written by two widely respected linguists who are well known for their detailed analysis of language in the community.

They take a topic which is regarded as a problem by very large numbers of people: the view that some forms of language are 'correct', that others are 'incorrect', and that the correct forms should be prescribed. Many linguists have regarded such a view as rather silly and beneath their contempt. But how could it be unimportant? It is a very widespread view which has existed for hundreds of years, in many different places; people constantly write to the newspapers or the BBC to complain about language usage; and teachers have to make appropriate judgments every time they read a pupil's essay which contains 'mistakes'. Linguists cannot simply ignore speakers' views of their own language.

The problem is usually conceived as one of standards. But *standard* is a very ambiguous term. It is not at all obvious that *standard* means the same thing in, for example, the *gold standard*, *standard of living* and *Standard English*. And whilst, in everyday thinking, *standards* are something good which should be maintained, *standardisation* is often seen as bad. (The authors are not, incidentally, attacking Standard English, nor arguing that it should not be taught in schools. Though, as they themselves remark, they may be misinterpreted in this way – such is the conceptual confusion in this area.)

This book provides a careful historical and contemporary commentary on the problem of prescription. Whereas many people just complain about (declining) standards, the authors of this book analyse the conceptual confusions which lead to much of the difficulty. They distinguish between speech and writing, between the language system itself and the way it is used, between individual usage and community norms, between linguistic and social value judgments, and they analyse the variation and change inherent in languages. They admit that some of the confusions are due to linguists in the past who have ignored issues of social importance and have not taken seriously their responsibility to debate the issues which are felt to be important by most people. Therefore they both reconsider long-held academic beliefs about language, in the light of social issues; and also apply linguistic knowledge carefully and rationally to the analysis of a social problem.

The book should be of great value and interest to all teachers and other educationalists, since the relation between Standard English and the education system is close, though complex. It should be of practical use to all those, such as speech therapists, who are involved in assessing linguistic development: the authors have very precise recommendations to make here. And it should also be of interest to everyone who has either written to the newspapers to complain

about some pet linguistic hate, or who has read such a letter, and
agreed with it, or been exasperated by its lack of rationality.

Michael Stubbs
Nottingham

Preface

It is well known that in British and American society judgments are made about 'correct' and 'incorrect' use of English and that in some countries, such as France and Italy, academies exist which prescribe 'correct' use of the language concerned. In this book, it is our intention to examine such prescriptive judgments about language and the consequences of such judgments in society and in the daily lives of individuals. We attempt to do this in a wide historical and social context.

First, we consider some difficulties in assessing popular and publicly expressed attitudes to language use, and we relate prescriptive attitudes to the phenomenon of language standardisation. This entails a consideration of the historical development of standard English and the consequences of this in eighteenth-century prescriptivism. We also attempt to consider the mechanisms by which the notion of a standard language has been maintained, and in Chapter 2 we give special attention to a linguistic complaint tradition in English. This tradition, which has taken the form of complaint about so-called mis-use of language and linguistic decline, has altered little since the eighteenth century.

Second, we attempt a critique of some forms of prescriptivism. In this critique, we point out that, although standard languages are necessary and must be maintained, many of the narrower forms of prescriptivism have lost sight of the function of prescription in maintaining the standard. Our argument involves making some necessary distinctions that are often not made (for example, the distinction between speech and writing and between 'grammaticality' and 'acceptability' in language use). We have also found it necessary to point out the wide capacity of ordinary individuals who use language appropriately in a variety of different circumstances − their communicative competence.

Finally, we look at some of the practical consequences of language prescription and standardisation in formal teaching and language testing. We attempt to demonstrate that in professional contexts such as language teaching and speech therapy, prescriptive ideologies have a considerable effect on the design and scoring of language assessment procedures, and that such procedures are often inadequate. Our critique of such procedures is based on the facts of language variation and communicative competence as we have discussed them in earlier chapters.

The first two chapters are concerned with the relation of prescription to standardisation of language, and to mechanisms by which standardisation is maintained. Chapters 3 and 4 consider the distinction between speech and writing and the tendency of prescriptive statements to be based purely on written language, taking little account of variation in speech. Chapter 5 looks more closely at the social stratification of language that results partly from standardisation. Chapters 6 and 7 extend the discussion to *communicative competence*, arguing that the language abilities of speakers need to be defined in terms of their capacity to use a number of styles and varieties appropriately; prescription, however, is characteristically confined to judgments on a single specific style or variety. In Chapter 8 we look more closely at the effects of prescription on language assessment procedures.

It will be clear from this brief summary that we examine practical consequences of language prescription and standardisation primarily from the perspective of recent empirical, descriptive and theoretical work in *linguistics*, including *sociolinguistics*. As far as possible we have attempted to exclude prior ideological commitment – i.e. our approach has not been developed within any particular socio-political theoretical paradigm.

The book is the joint work of both authors. The main drafts of Chapters 1–4 were prepared by J. Milroy, and those of Chapters 5–8 by L. Milroy. Both authors have, however, been fully involved in the organisation and preparation of all parts of the book, and they take joint responsibility for its contents. As there has recently been considerable public discussion of language problems in such spheres as the educational system, we hope that this book will help to extend the debate.

We are grateful to the following friends and colleagues for comments and criticisms on an earlier draft of the book. We appreciate their help, while of course taking full responsibility for the version which now appears in print. Thanks to Kevin Connolly, Anthony Edwards, Paul Fletcher, Michael McTear, William Mittins, Katherine Perera, Don Porter and John Wilson; to our series editor Michael Stubbs we are particularly grateful for comment, advice and support, and for the idea of writing the book in the first place.

To the Speech Therapists of Northern Ireland and the Speech Therapy students of the Ulster Polytechnic, with whom the ideas set out in Chapter 8 were developed during the years 1978–82, particular thanks are due. We are also extremely grateful for the generosity of the Simon Committee of the University of Manchester, who enabled Lesley Milroy to work on the manuscript of this book during her tenure of the Senior Simon Fellowship in 1982–3. The support of colleagues in the Department of General Linguistics, University of Manchester, during this period, is also much appreciated. We are also grateful to Josie Barber, Ted Cornell and Nicola Nash (of the Department of Linguistics, University of Sheffield) for help with preparation of the typescript. Finally, thanks to Graham McGregor for help with proofreading.

James Milroy
University of Sheffield

Lesley Milroy
University of
Newcastle upon Tyne

Key to symbols and abbreviations used in the text

Phonetic symbols are enclosed in square brackets, e.g. [a]; they indicate pronunciation of given sounds.

Phonemic symbols are enclosed in slant brackets, e.g. /a/; they are used to indicate contrasts in sound – thus, /a/ in *bat* and other words contrasts with /ɛ/ in *bet* and other words.

Where phonetic and phonemic symbols are not self-explanatory, their values are exemplified in keywords.

Linguistic variables, as defined by sociolinguistic investigators, are enclosed in round brackets, e.g. (a).

Citations of *spelling forms* are italicised; thus, *h* refers to a letter and not necessarily to any corresponding sound.

Abbreviations used are explained in the text. The main ones are:

RP	Received Pronunciation
SE	Standard English
NSE	Non-standard English
BEV	Black English Vernacular

1
Prescription and standardisation

1.1 Language prescription and its consequences

In this book we attempt to look dispassionately at *prescription* in language and the effects of prescriptive attitudes on the daily lives of individuals. Prescription depends on an ideology (or set of beliefs) concerning language which requires that in language use, as in other matters, things shall be done in the 'right' way. We can, perhaps, best understand what it is by comparing language with other aspects of human behaviour, such as dress or table manners. If, in a particular culture at a particular time, guests at a dinner are required to wear evening dress (of a particular form) and required to use their knives and forks in a particular way, these requirements are *prescriptive*, that is, they are imposed from 'above' by 'society', not by *ad hoc* agreement amongst the guests themselves. They are also *arbitrary*: in North America, for example, the fork is transferred to the right hand for eating, whereas in Britain, the fork remains in the left hand and the knife in the right. One could actually think of a variety of perfectly efficient ways – besides these – in which a meal could be eaten; yet, in these cultures, the slightest deviation from the prescribed norms is immediately noticed and considered to be 'bad manners'.

Language is a much more complex phenomenon than table manners: it is also a much more central aspect of human experience. Whereas table manners are codified in handbooks of etiquette, 'correct' use of language is codified in handbooks of usage. It is probable that all speakers of English (and probably most speakers of many other languages) have a number of definite opinions as to what is 'correct' or 'incorrect' in the language they use. They may often look to 'expert' opinion, rather than to their own knowledge of the language, to decide. Particular English usages, such as double negatives, as in *He never said nothing*, are viewed as unacceptable although they are very widely used; some varieties of a language (e.g. BBC spoken English) are publicly considered to be 'better' than some other varieties (e.g. Birmingham urban dialect). Indeed, some languages are thought to be in some senses 'better' than others: it has often been claimed for example that French is more logical than English.

Language, as we have suggested, is a much more complex phenomenon than such things as table manners, and it is difficult to separate the nature of language prescription (i.e. imposition of norms of usage by authority) from a number of related phenomena, such as *normalisation* and *standardisation* of language. In this first chapter, we shall attempt to address these difficulties; in particular we shall relate prescriptive attitudes very largely to standardisation of language. However, we must first briefly consider some of the consequences of prescriptive and authoritarian attitudes to language behaviour for the daily lives of individuals. These consequences are more wide-ranging than has usually been acknowledged, and it is part of our purpose in this book to indicate how deeply these attitudes affect us and how widespread their consequences are.

Some of the narrower consequences of language prescription are really quite well known, although they are usually accepted by the public as quite reasonable and are not questioned. A person who speaks English perfectly effectively, but who has occasional usages that are said to be 'substandard' (e.g. omitting initial [h] in words like *happy*, *hair*, or using double negatives) may well find that his/her social mobility is blocked and may, for example, be refused access to certain types of employment without any official admission that the refusals depend partly or wholly on his use of language. This point is quite clearly understood by the writer of the following (a Victorian English language scholar), who spoke of [h] dropping as a 'revolting habit', and added:

> Those whom we call 'self-made men' are much given to this hideous barbarism....Few things will the English youth find in after-life more profitable than the right use of the aforesaid letter. (Oliphant, 1873:226)

These are strong words; yet many readers may believe that it is quite right that people should be refused employment on the grounds of 'wrong' pronunciation or grammar *alone*, possibly justifying this opinion by arguing that these faults are signs of 'carelessness', which reflect on the general character of the individual. They may not, however, be aware that a majority of their fellow-citizens are accustomed to commit 'faults' (such as [h]-dropping), and that they are, therefore, condemning a very large proportion of the population. Furthermore, those who do use so-called 'unacceptable' grammar and pronunciation generally belong to the lower social groups; therefore, such attitudes to language can be interpreted as a kind of social-class discrimination, and it may be that political power favouring certain élite groups is exercised in part through these shibboleths. Although public discrimination on the grounds of race, religion and social class is not now publicly acceptable, it appears that discrimination on linguistic grounds *is* publicly acceptable, even though linguistic differences may themselves be associated with ethnic, religious and class differences (see further J. R. Edwards, 1979; Hudson, 1980). These attitudes to the use of grammar and pronunciation are, in any case, highly interesting in themselves and will be further discussed below.

As a result of the development of sociolinguistic research in recent years, it has become possible to address a number of practical problems in social and educational matters that can be affected by prescriptive attitudes to language. Two of these are particularly discussed in this book. The first arises from the fact that many 'advanced' countries, including Britain, now have much larger non-indigenous populations than they had in the first half of the century. Britain is now a multi-cultural and a multi-lingual society (for some details and a discussion, see Linguistic Minorities Project 1985), and a large number of different mother-tongues are used in Britain. The necessity for the major language (English) to be accessible to non-indigenous groups is not the only consequence arising.

Sociolinguistic research has, amongst other things, tried to identify the cultural and social disadvantages that are encountered by these groups in acquiring and using the majority language. But there have also been important researches into the difficulties encountered by members of minority groups in public and social transactions (which always involve the use of language). These difficulties, it has become clear, are not confined to mastering the vocabulary, grammar and segmental phonology (pronunciation of vowels and consonants) of English. They may, for instance, affect intonation of utterances; if it happens that the intonation of polite questions in the mother-tongue is similar to that of commands in English, the non-native speaker may be thought to be behaving rudely when he uses that intonation. In a broader sense, it has been shown that there are different cultural norms of politeness and different expectations as to language use in different speech events and transactions, e.g. in employment interviews (Furnborough *et al.*, 1982). Sometimes, because of these different cultural expectations, the non-native interviewee may be thought to be over-respectful and ingratiating; at other times he may appear to be sullen and awkward because the norms of his own culture require that he should not appear over-confident and 'pushy' in such situations. This can result in a poor opinion of the interviewee on the part of the interview board, and a sense of grievance (leading to accusations of racial discrimination) on the part of the candidate. To the extent that cultural norms (intermingled as they are in these cases with linguistic norms) are prescriptive, these matters can be embraced in a sociolinguistic view of the ideology of language prescription (see Chapter 6 for further discussion).

A second extended area in which the prescriptive ideology is important is language testing and assessment. Standardised tests that are intended to estimate children's linguistic abilities are used in the educational systems of many countries, including Britain and the United States. Standardised testing procedures are also widely used to assess degrees of language handicap in people (often children) who have speech impairments. This is not an unimportant matter. It was estimated by Quirk (1972) that about 4 per cent of a population is likely to suffer from language handicap: this means that the number of speech-impaired people in Britain is probably over 2 million.

Language testing and assessment, as we shall demonstrate in Chapter 7, are often based on rather simplistic notions of the nature of language and its use. The tests frequently do not take account of variation according to dialect and occasion of use. In addition, they often do not allow for the application of conversational rules such as ellipsis. Thus, if a child is shown a picture of a horse jumping over a fence and asked what the horse is doing, he may be penalised for replying: *Jumping over a fence* rather than *The horse is jumping over a fence*, despite the fact he is applying a normal conversation rule of ellipsis. He may then be given a lower score, which might not greatly distinguish him in this case from a child at an earlier stage of speech development who answers *Horse jump fence.* In such cases, it seems that the test procedure is confusing literary or written norms (which are resistant to ellipsis) with spoken norms (see further, Chapters 3, 4 and 8 below).

We have argued that prescriptive attitudes have far-reaching consequences including the two already mentioned, and these consequences are explored in some detail in later chapters. But, in the remainder of this chapter, we are concerned more broadly with the nature of language prescription and its relation to the process of language standardisation. In Section 2 we go on to discuss the attitudes of professional language scholars to prescription and compare these (in Section 3) with public and popular attitudes. In the final section we attempt a fuller account of the nature of language standardisation.

1.2   Linguistics and prescription

The existence of prescriptive attitudes is well known to linguistic scholars, but in 'mainstream' linguistics of recent times scholars have generally claimed that prescription is not a central part of their discipline and even that it is irrelevant to linguistics. It has not been fully studied as an important sociolinguistic phenomenon. All standard introductory textbooks in linguistics affirm that linguistics is a descriptive discipline and not a prescriptive one:

> First, and most important, linguistics is *descriptive*, not prescriptive. A linguist is interested in what *is* said, not what he thinks *ought* to be said. He describes language in all its aspects, but does not prescribe rules of 'correctness'. (Aitchison, 1978:13)

Similarly, handbooks compiled by linguistic scholars make the same reservations. Daniel Jones has this to say in the introduction to his *English Pronouncing Dictionary* (1955): 'No attempt is made to decide how people *ought* to pronounce; all that the dictionary aims at doing is to give a faithful record of the manner in which certain people do pronounce.'

Although it is necessary to insist on the priority of description, it does not follow from this that prescription should never be studied at any point. However, the reservation about prescription that is commonly expressed has, in practice, led to a general tendency to study language *as if* prescriptive phenomena play no part in language. Many professional language scholars appear to feel that, whereas it is respectable to write formal grammars, it is not quite respectable to study prescription.

The attitudes of linguists (professional scholars of language) have little or no effect on the general public, who continue to look to dictionaries, grammars and handbooks as authorities on 'correct' usage. If, for example, lexicographers (dictionary-makers) attempt to remove all traces of value-judgment from their work and refuse to label particular usages (such as *ain't*) as 'colloquial' and others as 'slang', there is likely to be a public outcry. This was notoriously the case when *Webster's Third New International Dictionary* appeared in the USA in 1961 (see the discussion by Sledd, 1962). Its failure to provide such evaluations of usage was described by one critic as 'a scandal and a disaster': behind such attitudes one can sense the view that since the language is believed to be always on a downhill path, it is up to experts (such as dictionary-makers) to arrest and reverse the decline. It is not necessary to dwell at length on these widely shared attitudes. Readers will have seen letters to the newspapers complaining about particular usages, and we shall comment later on the 'complaint tradition' in English.

Modern linguistic scholars, however, have always had good reason to assert that their discipline is fundamentally descriptive and not prescriptive. During this century, their assertions have been motivated by a desire to study language in all its forms as objectively as possible. If we want to know more about language as a phenomenon and the universal human capacity to use it, then we must try to base our discipline on observed fact (as far as possible) and certainly not on a set of prejudices. After all (so the argument runs), it would be absurd for a physical scientist to refuse to study some molecule because he felt it was more 'sloppy' or 'careless' than some other molecule or for a zoologist to classify animals in terms of their 'ugliness' or 'friendliness' rather than their membership of genera, etc.; it is equally absurd for the linguist to rule out study of some particular aspect of language use because he has some negative attitude to it. In this view of linguistics, the idea of linguistics as a 'science' obiously looms very large.

The view that linguistics is a science (bound up as it is with anti-prescriptive and anti-evaluative notions) has been prominent for a much longer time than is generally acknowledged; it was quite clearly stated in the nineteenth century. In 1861, the first volume of Max Müller's *Lectures on the Science of Language* appeared. In the first chapter, Müller stated that linguistics was a *physical* science. In this, he was affected by current nineteenth-century notions of the nature of science: he meant that linguistics was analogous to biology and geology and differentiated from 'humanities' such as history, literature and law (1861:22). Müller went on to make the usual assertion that all forms of language are equal as far as the 'scientist' is concerned:

> In the science of languages.... language itself becomes the sole object of scientific inquiry. Dialects which have never produced any literature at all.... are as important, nay for the solution of some of our problems, more important, than the poetry of Homer, or the prose of Cicero. (1861:23)

Before this time, Richard Chenevix Trench (1851) (who later became an archbishop) had proclaimed that language had its own 'life', independent of man, and had attacked those who attempted to control the development of language by 'arbitrary decrees' (Trench, 1888:223–4). These nineteenth-century scholars were themselves reacting against the authoritarian linguistics of the eighteenth century, which we discuss later in this volume. For nineteenth-century scholars, linguistics had become primarily a historical or evolutionary discipline. It was clearly necessary for them to give attention to obscure and antique varieties of a 'non-standard' kind if they were to explain the complicated processes of change that had given rise to modern languages like French, English and German, and which continued to affect these languages.

Although these respectable Victorians were already reacting strongly against the prescriptive attitudes of the eighteenth century, the most extreme anti-prescriptive statements, as far as we know, are those made by some members of the 'American structuralist' school of linguistics. Bloomfield (1933:22) felt that discovering why *ain't* is considered bad and *am not* good is not a fundamental question in linguistics, and he thought it strange that 'people without linguistic training' should devote 'a great deal of effort to futile discussions of this topic'. Bloomfield was certainly implying that the study of prescriptivism was of little or no interest to linguistics; he was thereby limiting the field of linguistics to a descriptive study of form and system in language which takes little or no account of language as a *social* phenomenon. Bloomfield's influence has been immense, and some of his followers have attacked 'unscientific' approaches to language with missionary zeal. C. C.

Fries (1957) seems to have equated traditional school grammar with prescription (which was by definition 'bad' and 'unscientific' in the view of structural linguists of the time), and in his book on English syntax he went so far as to even reject traditional linguistic terms such as 'noun', 'verb' and 'adjective'. Fries's work was directed towards the educational system; that of Robert A. Hall, Jr. was directed at the ordinary consumer. Anxious to assure all his readers that their use of language was just as good as that of anyone else, he proclaimed that 'there is no such thing as good or bad, correct or incorrect, grammatical or ungrammatical, in language' (1950).

Although linguistic scholars would now dispute Hall's statement (especially the part about 'grammatical or ungrammatical'), they have continued (for the most part) to assert or assume that their discipline is descriptive and theoretical and that they do not deal in prescription. In Western Europe and America most theoretical linguists would still affirm that all forms of language are in principle equal. As Hudson (1980:191) has recently put it:

> Linguists would claim that if they were simply shown the grammars of two different varieties, one with high and the other with low prestige, they could not tell which was which, any more than they could predict the skin colour of those who speak the two varieties.

Although some evidence from work by social psychologists (Giles *et al.*, 1974, 1975) lends some support to Hudson's point, we do not, in fact, know whether *standard* languages can be conclusively shown to have *no* purely linguistic characteristics that differentiate them from non-standard forms of language (the matter has not really been investigated). It appears to be an article of faith at the moment that judgments evaluating differences between standard and non-standard varieties are always socially conditioned and never purely linguistic. However, we shall later suggest that the process of language standardisation involves *the suppression of optional variability in language* and that, as a consequence, non-standard varieties can be observed to permit more variability than standard ones (e.g. in pronunciations of particular words). Thus, there may be one sense at least in which the *linguistic* characteristics of non-standard varieties differ from those of 'standards'.

However this may be, we shall see in Chapter 4 that non-standard forms are not simply debased variants of standards and that they can be shown to be 'grammatical' in their own terms.

Historically, standard languages have been superimposed on dialects. If a linguistic scholar is to do his work adequately (to give a clear description of a language, to explain how children acquire language, to explain how languages change in the course of time), he would be extremely foolish to allow his own prejudices and notions of correctness to get between him and his data. But the professional linguist's insistence on 'objectivity' and 'scientific inquiry' appears to have been generally misunderstood. This may arise partly from scholarly neglect (until recently) of the *social* functions of language. Although it is understandable that linguists should have to place clear limitations on their field of inquiry (especially if they are to make progress in *formal* linguistics, following Chomsky (1965) etc.), we are unlikely to make great progress in understanding the nature of language if we entirely ignore its *social* functions and characteristics. Amongst these are phenomena such as language standardisation, the nature of literacy, notions of prestige in language and popular attitudes to usage.

In the following sections, we shall go on to consider such matters. But first we should like to point out that misunderstanding of linguists' attacks on prescription may have had dire consequences in some quarters. Since the 1950s there has been a decline in the teaching of 'grammar' in schools. Some educationalists appear to have interpreted attacks on *prescriptive* grammar as attacks on the teaching of grammar in general; and as university language teachers, we have become aware that some students now enter universities to study English or modern languages with a rather hazy idea of basic grammatical terminology (such as *subject, transitive, preposition*). Some commentators have even claimed that there has been a decline in general literacy as a result of this trend. We see no reason to accept this latter point, as it is a relative question that cannot be adequately tested. However, experts in linguistics have sometimes been blamed for the decline in grammar teaching (and the supposed decline in literacy).

Recently Honey (1983) has asserted that English language teaching has been in decline, and has gone on to blame the discipline of linguistics for this decline. No reason is given for the connection that Honey makes between literacy standards and the influence of general linguists (such as Chomsky), and the author does not make the necessary distinction between language *system* and language *use* (on which see Section 3).

The quotations from linguists that Honey gives (largely to the effect that 'all languages are equal') refer to language *system* and not to the *use* of language in social context. In fact, many linguistic scholars have been at the forefront of those who have wished to maintain good educational standards (Stubbs and Hillier, 1983; Sinclair, 1982) and they have made *positive* recommendations for improved language work in schools.

The authors of elementary books on linguistics, however, have usually been anxious to dissociate their account of the subject from that of traditional handbooks of correctness. As we have seen (cf Aitchison, above) they usually dismiss prescription routinely, and assert that linguistics is *descriptive*. Their general point − that, if one is to study the nature of language objectively, one cannot make prior value-judgments − is frequently misunderstood, and it has sometimes called forth splenetic and misinformed denunciations of linguistics as a whole. One example amongst many is Simon (1980).

In an essay entitled 'The Corruption of English' (1980), Simon blames structural linguistics and literary structuralists for an alleged decline in language use and for permissive attitudes to language: 'What this is, masquerading under the euphemism "descriptive linguistics", ... is a benighted and despicable catering to mass ignorance under the supposed aegis of democracy.' His essay is outspoken and full of emotive language ('pseudoscientific mumbo jumbo', 'rock-bottom illiteracy', 'barbarians', 'vandalism', etc.), and it betrays ignorance of what linguistics is about. To Simon, linguists are almost equated with some menace that is threatening Western (i.e. American) civilisation from outside. It is unfortunate that misunderstandings and misapplications of the American structural linguists' teaching should have made it seem reasonable for anyone to write in this ignorant way.

As many people still interpret descriptive linguistics as inimical to standards of usage, there has clearly been some failure of communication between linguistic scholars and the general public (especially when we consider that scholars have been insisting on objective description for so long − since the time of Trench and Müller). One reason for this is that 'mainstream' linguistics (especially in the USA) has concentrated more on the abstract and formal properties of language than on language in its social context. Bloomfield (1933), as we saw above, considered that prescription was irrelevant to linguistics as a 'science'. Yet some linguists (relatively few) have been directly interested in prescription. Haas

(1982), for example, has been able to state that prescription 'is an integral part of the life of language'. By refusing to be interested in prescription, he adds: 'linguists only ensure that every enterprise of linguistic planning will be dominated by ignorant enthusiasts and incompetent pedants' (Haas, 1982:3).

The development of sociolinguistics in recent years has awakened a greater interest (than used to be fashionable) in text-based linguistics, standardisation of language and the general nature of variation and change in language. When we view language as fundamentally a social phenomenon, we cannot then ignore prescription and its consequences. The study of linguistic authoritarianism is an important part of linguistics, and as linguists we feel an obligation to attempt to close the gap between specialist and non-specialist views on the nature and use of language. One reason for this is that attitudes to language have practical consequences, for example in education, law, business and speech therapy. But the best reason for studying prescription is simply that it is interesting in itself.

1.3 Attitudes to language

As we saw in the last section, the attitudes to language expressed by many people are *prescriptive*, whereas scholars usually take the view that linguistics is a *descriptive* 'science' which has no place for value-judgments. In this section, we explore this difference a little further, but, in addition, we should like to suggest that public attitudes as they are openly expressed may not always be identical with the views that people hold privately. Bolinger (1980:1–10) has had much to say about what he calls linguistic *shamanism*: he has noted that certain writers set themselves up as public guardians of usage, commenting on supposed mis-use of language and on supposed linguistic decline. These statements by guardians appear frequently in the press; general 'popular' attitudes (i.e. privately held attitudes of ordinary people), however, may not be quite so easily accessible for reasons we shall discuss. In what follows, we shall first explore further the differences between the approach of linguistics and the public judgments of non-linguists, and then pass on to point out certain difficulties in reconciling these public views with the actual speech behaviour of ordinary speakers.

Modern linguistics, following de Saussure (1915), is based on the doctrine of the arbitrariness of the linguistic sign, and progress in the subject would have been very difficult without this doctrine. As de Saussure perceived, the linguistic forms that conventionally stand for things in the real world do not ultimately bear a necessary and inherent relationship to those referents. Thus, the sound sequence in the English word *dog* bears no inherent relationship to the canine quadruped it refers to: it is merely conventional to use this item in English to refer to the animal. Even echoic or onomatopoeic words differ in different languages, e.g. *cock-a-doodle-doo*, *kikiriki*. It would be foolish to argue that an English usage such as *dog* is somehow a 'better' or 'worse' way of referring to the canine than equivalents in other languages, such as *chien* or *Hund*. Similarly, it would be foolish to argue that *in general* the grammatical structure of one language is 'superior' to that of another. The word-order of English (in which the subject precedes the verb) is not superior to that of Gaelic (in which the verb comes first): it is merely different, and neither word-order is directly conditioned by relationship to 'the real world'. In short, if one wishes to produce accurate descriptions, one cannot reasonably start by making value-judgments about the formal grammatical, lexical and phonological structures of different languages or dialects (e.g. by rejecting or ignoring some features that are pre-judged as not 'acceptable' to some analyst or other). One consequence of the doctrine of arbitrariness is the linguist's working assumption that no language or dialect can be shown to be better or worse than another *on linguistic grounds alone*.

Ordinary people (i.e. non-linguists), however, have been accustomed from time immemorial to make value judgments about language. Words have even been considered to have magical properties or have been subject to tabu. Certain words referring, for example, to the deity, illness, sex, death, may be forbidden, and in some societies a man is not allowed to use his mother-in-law's name. Certain words associated with bodily functions are avoided in most circumstances and replaced by euphemisms such as *wee-wee* or, in formal circumstances, by technical terms such as *faeces*, *vagina*. The histories of languages are full of rapid vocabulary changes motivated by the avoidance of tabu, as the euphemisms themselves take on the 'unpleasant' associations of the words they replace. All this may seem to be very illogical, but it is part of the life of language. The ordinary user of language does not, apparently, agree with Shakespeare's common-sense observation: 'that which we call a rose by any other name would smell as sweet', and he may also feel that the words of his language have inherent associations with the things they stand for. As the farm-hand observed while he watched the pigs wallowing in the mire 'Rightly be they called pigs on account of their disgusting habits'.

Apart from beliefs in magic, tabu and the 'power of words', there are other firmly held opinions about language that do not accept the linguist's doctrine of arbitrariness. Many of these have to do with social stratification and cultural conditioning. Some dialects of a language are considered more 'beautiful' than others; some languages are widely held to be more 'logical' than others. We shall later consider these attitudes and their consequences in greater detail. For the moment, let us accept that although the formal structures of languages and dialects are not appropriate phenomena for value-judgments, speakers of languages *do* attach values to particular words, grammatical structures and speech-sounds. There is apparently a yawning gap between what linguists profess to think about language and what ordinary people assume in their daily use and observation of language.

We have referred above to the 'formal structures' of languages, implying a distinction between this 'formal structure' and the actual use of language on particular occasions. A distinction of this kind has been basic in the work of most general linguists since de Saussure proposed a distinction between *langue* (approximately 'language system') and *parole* (approximately 'language use'). A similar distinction was proposed by Chomsky (1965) as *competence* (the underlying rules of language that native speakers know) and *performance* (actual 'use'). It is important to grasp that *langue, competence* or 'language system' are relatively abstract: in practice, many of the most influential thinkers in linguistics have been concerned with this abstract 'language system'. They have been more interested in trying to explain the universal human ability to acquire language and master its complexities than in value-judgments about particular usages: it is not surprising that disputes about *ain't* and *between you and I* have seemed trivial to them, when they have been preoccupied with the fact that the general structure of all languages and dialects is so astonishingly complex. Public statements about language, however, always refer directly to language in use: they almost never show explicit understanding of the distinction between *system* and *use* and seldom acknowledge another important fact about language, viz., that it is in a continuous state of change.

Occasionally, however, guardians do make claims based on

actual *usage* that nevertherless contain implicit claims about the
superiority of one language *system* over another. An article by
Boyd and Boyd (1980) has suggested that varieties of English that
distinguish between *shall* and *will* have an advantage over those
that have only *will* in so far as they have an additional resource that
can give added subtlety and precision. Interesting as such
arguments are, it is our view that they are misleading. All languages
and dialects will, when compared with others, appear to have
'gaps' in the system at some point. For example, English does not
have a reflexive possessive pronoun. We do not say:

*Sam is in himself's office.

If we use an anaphoric pronoun (one that refers back to an antecedent), we must say:

Sam is in his office.

This is ambiguous when out of context, as *his office* could be
'Sam's office' or some other male person's office. In other
languages, the system may have an additional resource and may
require a choice at this point between reflexive and non-reflexive.
Thus, in Danish:

Sam er i *sit* kontor

means – unambiguously – 'Sam is in Sam's office', whereas

Sam er i *hans* kontor

means that Sam is in someone else's office. It is pointless to argue
that English *ought* to have a possessive reflexive pronoun like
Danish *sin, sit*; it is, in fact, quite easy to use other resources of the
language system to disambiguate when necessary. We can say either
Sam is in his own office or *Sam is in Bill's office*. The gap in the
system, therefore, is not necessarily a problem in the actual use of
the language.

Indeed, the argument that *shall/will* dialects of English (generally regarded as standard varieties) have the advantage over *will*
dialects (generally non-standard) can easily be matched by
arguments that non-standard dialects have other similar advantages
over the standard. For example, the *language system* of Standard
English has no grammatical resource for differentiating between
singular and plural in the second person pronoun (*you*). Some
dialects, however, have a categorical distinction between *you*

(singular) and *yous* (plural). In such dialects (e.g. Northern Irish), a comment like *I'll see you tomorrow* will be understood to be directed to only one person in a given group: *I'll see yous tomorrow* will, however, be preferred when two or more persons in the company are addressed. This appears to be a useful resource in these non-standard dialects (even though the standard speaker can disambiguate when necessary by saying 'all of you' or something of the sort). But it is noticeable that guardians of the language do not generally recommend the 'superior' systems of non-standard dialects: they confine their claims about superiority to aspects of *standard* English grammar (such as the *shall/will* distinction). It can be suggested therefore, that their real concerns are not wholly linguistic but largely social: they are in some way promoting the interests of the variety most widely considered to have prestige.

At the level of *language system*, arguments that one language or dialect is linguistically superior to another are generally very difficult to sustain. The number and complexity of grammatical rules in any language or dialect cannot be easily shown to be significantly more or less than in some other language or dialect, and greater number and complexity of rules would not in any case prove superiority. General linguists, therefore, believe that it is pointless to argue in these terms. Considerations of *superiority* or *inferiority*, *beauty* or *ugliness* and *logicality* or *illogicality* in usage are held to be irrelevant at the level of *language system*, although they may be relevant at the level of use.

If claims about the superiority of one language to another are not amenable to rigorous proof, then neither can we prove that one language is *equal* to another. In a scientific academic context, this latter proposition is best viewed as a statement of the *null hypothesis*. But neither this claim nor the claim about superiority is in fact capable of satisfactory verification or falsification: the two claims are simply two sides of the same coin, and as they are popularly conceived and debated, they are ideological, rather than scientific, statements.

Those who argue about linguistic superiority may however sometimes point out that some languages appear to spread at the expense of others and to survive as others die out. English in Britain, for example, has spread at the expense of Celtic languages, and in Australia, aboriginal languages are threatened by English. Is this not a sign that English is a superior language? Again, there is no way of demonstrating that, at the level of language system,

English is indeed a superior language. The grammatical systems of these other languages are at least equally subtle and complex. The spread of English is due, not to its superiority as a system of language, but to the greater economic and political success of its speakers in recent centuries. In a similar way, Classical Latin became the official language of a great empire; yet, its great prestige did not ensure its ultimate survival in the face of political and economic change.

Language guardians do not usually make explicit reference to the distinction between *language system* and *language use*. Their comments usually focus on certain particular points of usage (e.g. the *shall/will* distinction or the double negative). Thus they appear to be comments about language use rather than system. Yet these comments often have implications for language system, as appeals for preferring one usage over another are often based on some limited aspect of language system (e.g. analogy with other grammatical constructions in the language). To demonstrate the kind of argumentation that is used, we shall discuss the prescription in favour of *different from* as against *different to* – a prescription that seems to have originated in the eighteenth century, but which is still found in handbooks of correctness (e.g. Metcalfe, 1975).

In this construction the choice of *from* or *to* is *arbitrary* in the sense that the selection of one or the other makes no difference to the meaning of the construction. Clearly, in other circumstances, the choice of *from* or *to* is not arbitrary, but meaningful, as in *John ran to the house* as against *John ran from the house*. The directional particles in these sentences have *contrastive* meanings. In *different from* and *different to*, however, the particles *from* and *to* seem in effect to have lost their usual meanings and to have become empty connectors: the construction has the same meaning regardless of whether *from* or *to* is used (see Hurford and Heasley, 1983:50 for a discussion of 'meaningless' and 'meaningful' prepositions).

Various arguments can be used to justify the choice of one construction as against the other. In favour of *different from*, we can argue on the analogy of the verb *differ*, which requires the particle *from* and not *to*: we say *chalk differs from cheese* and not **chalk differs to cheese*. On the other hand, *different to* might be justified on the grounds that it falls into a set of words with comparative meanings such as *similar, equal, superior*, etc.: these require *to*, as in *similar to, equal to*. Furthermore, the eighteenth century could well have argued for *different to* by appealing to Latin grammar (as they commonly did in other circumstances): in Latin the verb 'to differ' takes the *dative* case after it, and this is translated into English as *to* or *for*. A third variant, *different than* (which is particularly common in Scotland, Ireland and North America), can also be justified on the analogy of certain comparative uses in English, such as *other than*, or even *better than*, *worse than*. Thus, there are three choices, all of which can be justified by some argument; yet the prescriptive tradition generally recommends that only one of these is 'correct' and should be selected in preference to the others.

In this discussion we have not been attempting to suggest that the handbook prescriptions should be overthrown and one of the 'disallowed' usages elevated to a position of correctness. We should merely like to emphasise two things. First, language guardians usually feel a strong compulsion to select one, and only one, from a set of equivalent usages and recommend that as the 'correct' form. Second, their choice of a preferred form is often arbitrary — in linguistic terms: the other variants are quite serviceable. Arguments that are advanced in support of the preferred form can usually be matched by equally good arguments in support of the rejected forms. But all these arguments are *post hoc* rationalisations, and do not in themselves prove anything. It is likely that eighteenth-century preference for *different from* rested, not on any real superiority in terms of logic, effectiveness, elegance or anything else, but on the observed usage of the 'best people' at that time. The choice of that particular form was probably *socially* motivated, and the general compulsion to select one form out of a set of equivalents was a consequence of the trend towards standardisation, a characteristic of which is the *suppression of optional variability* (see 1.4, below).

Apart from analogical arguments and arguments based on Latin grammar (e.g. 'never use a preposition at the end of a sentence'), language guardians have also used arguments based on *logic* or *mathematics* and on *etymology*. Thus, a mathematical argument ('two negatives make a positive') was used in the eighteenth century to condemn the double negative (as in *I never said nothing*), and etymological arguments are still very commonly used in matters of vocabulary. For example, it is held to be wrong to use *aggravating* in the sense 'annoying' as its Latin etymon means 'making heavier' (or 'more serious').

In Chapter 2 we go on to relate these publicly held views of correctness to the tradition of linguistic complaint in English and the place of the complaint tradition in the rise of Standard English. We now return to the difficult question of distinguishing between publicly expressed and privately held attitudes to social variation in language.

There is clearly a difficulty in relating publicly expressed attitudes to the views that ordinary people have of their own usage. First, so-called unacceptable usage and low-status varieties of language certainly persist despite being publicly stigmatised (Ryan, 1979). Presumably they could not persist if the relevant speakers felt strongly enough that they 'ought' to learn and use forms of higher prestige (on this see Chapter 3.1). Second, it seems to be virtually impossible to rely on speakers' reports of their own usage or of their attitudes to usage, so that we cannot easily find out what people actually think. Linguists and social psychologists who have investigated popular attitudes have found that people's overt claims about language are inaccurate and often contradict their own actual usage. As Labov (1972a:214) points out, speakers often err in the direction of standard usages when they respond to field-workers' questions about their own usage: they do not reliably report on what they use themselves. Labov (1966) also found that speakers with the 'broadest' pronunciations showed the greatest tendency to downgrade others for the same pronunciations. Socio-linguistic research has additionally shown that speakers certainly have *knowledge* of different variants (Glasgow speakers, for example, *know* that the medial consonant of the word *butter* alternates between [t] and the glottal stop): furthermore, they do not necessarily use the same variant 100 per cent of the time. Thus, if a speaker is observed to use *done* for *did* (as in *I done it*), it is quite likely that he also uses the *did* form some of the time. The fact that speakers have knowledge of variants and also knowledge of the social values attached to them means that speaker reports tend to indicate social stereotypes rather than personal or community values. They tend to report the form they consider to be socially accepted rather than the form they use themselves.

Some sociolinguists (Labov, 1966; Trudgill, 1974) have made use of 'Speaker-Report Tests' in order to estimate the reliability of speakers' claims about their own usage. Some speakers make what appear to be dishonest reports by claiming to use standard variants that they never actually use. In one study (O'Kane, 1977; J. Milroy, 1981), a number of working-class speakers in Belfast were given three different pronunciations of each of a series of common words like *hand*, *bag*, *stop*. The first pronunciation in each case was RP ('Received Pronunciation' – the 'Oxford' or 'BBC' accent), the second was 'general Belfast' and the third 'broad Belfast'. They were asked to say which one they used themselves. Several female respondents – all of them strongly non-standard speakers – claimed that they used the RP variant when it was plain that they *never* did. It appears that these speakers interpreted the task as a test of their knowledge of the 'correct' pronunciation and responded accordingly: they did not want to be thought ignorant.

These instances raise rather clearly the general problem of identifying popular attitudes. It seems that people are willing to pay lip-service to correctness and prestige variants, but at the same time they continue to speak the variety current in their own speech communities. In fact, statistical counts of variants actually used are probably the best way of assessing attitudes. Despite the views of the guardians, most people do not put into effect *absolute* views that particular usages are 'right' or 'wrong'. The work of Labov (1966) and others has, repeatedly, demonstrated that people feel some variants (e.g. [h]-less variants) to be appropriate in some 'styles' and other variants (e.g. [h]-ful ones) appropriate in other styles and contextual situations (for further discussion of this, see Chapter 5).

A major task of sociolinguistics is to explain why linguistic differences that are essentially arbitrary are assigned social values. Another associated task is to explain why people continue to use non-standard varieties when they claim publicly to agree that only the 'standard' is 'correct'. What is the function of prescriptive attitudes and what effects do they have?

This mismatch between actual usage and what people publicly claim to think constitutes one of the many paradoxes in sociolinguistics. But it is certainly clear that in the wider community there is some agreement that certain usages (phonological, grammatical and lexical) are stigmatised, whereas others carry prestige.

The histories of languages appear to contain many instances of contradictory and changing attitudes to the same arbitrary linguistic phenomenon. It is reasonable to ask why a characteristic like [h]-dropping has not always been stigmatised in all languages and dialects when it is so strongly stigmatised in present-day British English and dialects. In the Romance languages, for example, [h]-dropping cannot possibly have been stigmatised by all speakers in all communities at all times: if it had, these languages would have

retained Latin [h], but they have universally lost it. Obviously, it
would be foolish to accuse a French speaker of careless speech
because he fails to pronounce the *h* in *homme* 'when it is there in
the spelling'. The loss of [h] in Romance languages is a completed
linguistic change which must at certain times have been favoured
by influential social groups and so must have carried high prestige.

Even in English, it is unlikely that [h]-dropping was a matter of
public stigma much before 1800 (Wyld, 1927:211–12, 219), and
there are some signs that it may even have been socially favoured
in earlier centuries. There are many thirteenth- and fourteenth-
century texts that show considerable evidence of [h]-loss, and
Elizabethan puns often depend on [h]-loss (e.g. puns on *air/
hair/heir* in Marlowe, *Dido and Aeneas* and Shakespeare, *Comedy
of Errors*). Public stigma could hardly have been significant in
those centuries if [h]-dropping could appear in literary texts.
There is, therefore, a strong possibility that public attitudes to
[h]-dropping have been reversed. It seems that a usage favoured
at one time can become stigmatised at another (on the history of
[h]-dropping, see J. Milroy, 1983).

A very clear case of reversal in social evaluation is the case of the
post-vocalic [r] in New York City. Before the Second World War,
non-rhotic British accents and those of the American East Coast
had high status, and loss of post-vocalic [r] in words like *car*, *card*,
butter seems to have extended throughout the social class continuum in New York City. Labov's work demonstrates that by 1966
the loss of post-vocalic [r] had, on the contrary, become a marker
of casual style and lower social status, with formal styles and higher
status favouring rhotic forms. Thus it appears that in the USA
prestige forms are rhotic, whereas in England they are non-rhotic.
Clearly, these varying attitudes are social: in linguistic terms,
[h]-ful and [r]-ful accents are neither better nor worse than
[h]-less and [r]-less ones. The matter is arbitrary from the
linguistic point of view.

These phonological examples concern public evaluations of different resources of language systems. In England, dialects that lack
a systematic contrast between words with initial /h/ and words with
initial vowels (e.g. *hair* v. *air*) are accorded low status, whereas
dialects that lack a contrast between words with and without post-
vocalic /r/ (e.g. *court* v. *caught*) have high status. In grammatical
usage also it can be pointed out that the 'acceptability' or otherwise of particular variants is socially motivated and linguistically

arbitrary. To use *what* as a relative pronoun, as in *the house what I saw*, is neither more nor less efficient in terms of language system than to use SE *the house that I saw* or *the house which I saw* (see discussion in 3.4, 3.5). It is simply that some dialects use the item *what* as part of their relative pronoun system, while others (including SE) do not. In the next section and in subsequent chapters, we shall approach the question of arbitrary choices of this kind in terms of the ideology of standardisation.

Some readers may still feel that some types of usage can truly be shown to be better or worse than others – more logical, precise and effective perhaps, or less ambiguous or less vague. As we shall see, this is often correct at the level of *usage*. To evaluate usage as against *system*, however, depends on making a number of careful distinctions, of which the main one is the distinction between speech and writing. Prescriptive judgments and stigmatisation of particular forms have not normally made the necessary distinctions between *system* and *use*, or between speech and writing. Our major task here has been to point out that public statements condemning aspects of differing language systems do not make these distinctions clearly. Furthermore, they do not appear to have as much effect on ordinary speakers of non-standard English as one might expect. In the course of history, usages that were once publicly favoured have become stigmatised and usages that were stigmatised have become favoured. Indeed, it often happens that a particular usage is not attacked as non-standard until it has become very general and widespread. Margaret Thatcher was recently (1982) attacked for using the word *prevaricate* in the sense 'stall, play for time' when it should 'properly' mean 'tell lies'. In so doing, she used the word in the sense that most people now use it: the Latin etymology has been virtually lost (as it has been in thousands of other words), and the guardians in this case (as in many others) are locking the stable door after the horse has bolted. Linguistic change has overtaken them.

It is appropriate, therefore, to ask what is the function of the public guardians of usage if, in many cases of prescription of grammar, phonology and word-choice, their detailed recommendations go largely unheeded. In what follows, we shall make some distinctions that will go some way towards answering the question. Fundamentally, their role is related to the ideology of *standardisation*, in that they attempt to keep the notion of a standard language alive in the public mind. They are also, in many cases, genuinely and properly concerned with clarity and effectiveness in communication, but their prescriptions focus much more on public and written styles than on speech. Their recommendations may often be sensible in terms of written usage and well intended; but we shall see that a general failure to consider *spoken language* as against written language can have unfortunate consequences.

In Section 1.4 we pass on to a discussion of the nature of language standardisation (the consequences of which reflect strongly on the public and popular attitudes that we have discussed). In Chapter 2 we proceed to outline the history of standardisation of English and discuss some of the processes through which the notion of a standard language is maintained.

1.4 Language standardisation

For a number of reasons it is difficult to point to a fixed and invariant kind of English that can properly be called the standard language, unless we consider only the *written* form to be relevant. It is only in the spelling system that full standardisation really has been achieved, as deviations from the norm (however logical) are not tolerated there. When, however, we refer to 'standard' spoken English, we have to admit that a good deal of variety is tolerated in practice, and scholars have often had to loosen their definition of a 'standard' in dealing with speech. Thus it becomes possible for them to say that a standard form of English, which they believe to be largely uniform in its grammar and vocabulary, is nevertheless *spoken* in a variety of different *accents* (Quirk, 1968), or to speak of 'varieties of Standard English' (Trudgill and Hannah, 1982; cf. also Wyld's idea (1936) of a 'Modified Standard'). Strictly speaking, however, standardisation does not tolerate variability. Thus it is best, in our view, to look at the question of 'Standard English' in a different light, and to speak of standardisation as a historical process which – to a greater or lesser degree – is always in progress in those languages that undergo it. Standardisation is motivated in the first place by various social, political and commercial needs and is promoted in various ways, including the use of the writing system, which is relatively easily standardised; but absolute standardisation of a spoken language is never achieved (the only fully standardised language is a dead language). Therefore it seems appropriate to speak more abstractly of standardisation as an *ideology*, and a standard language as an idea in the mind rather than a reality – a set of abstract norms to which actual usage may conform to a greater or lesser extent.

If we consider standardisation in matters outside language, the notion applies rather obviously to other media of exchange, such as money, or weights and measures. Thus the coinage is strictly standardised so that there can be *no* variation in the values assigned to the counters in the system, and the aim of this standardisation is to ensure reliability and hence confidence. Language is also a medium of exchange, albeit a very much more complex medium than coinage, and the aim of language standardisation is the same. This was clear to the eighteenth-century writers on 'ascertainment': Swift (1712) was partly concerned with *improving* the language, but he preferred that the language (even if it was imperfect) should be standardised in a permanent form rather than it should be allowed to change continuously. Thus standardisation aims to ensure fixed values for the counters in a system. In language, this means preventing variability in spelling and pronunciation by selecting fixed conventions uniquely regarded as 'correct', establishing 'correct' meanings of words (*aggravate*, for example, means – according to the standard ideology – 'make more serious', not 'annoy': the second 'colloquial' meaning is disallowed), uniquely acceptable word-forms (*he does* is acceptable, but *he do* is not) and fixed conventions of sentence structure. The whole notion of standardisation is bound up with the aim of functional efficiency of the language. Ultimately, the desideratum is that everyone should use and understand the language in the same way with the minimum of misunderstanding and the maximum of efficiency.

This aim is wholly understandable, and many would argue that if the forms of a language were not validated and legitimised in some way by some authority or authorities, the language would break up into dialects that would sooner or later become mutually incomprehensible. This is what happened to late Latin after the collapse of the Roman Empire. As the central authority vanished, so the language fragmented into dialects which developed into the various Romance languages (French, Italian, Spanish, Portuguese, Romanian, Catalan, Friulian, Romansh and others). The ideology of standardisation requires not only that the English in the British Isles should be as uniform as possible, but also that it should be uniform in other places throughout the world where English has been implanted. Thus this ideology affects not only North America and Australasia, but also the English of, for example, Singapore (which has, in fact, diverged considerably from British English) and the Caribbean (for a discussion of Singapore English see Chapter 5).

In the strict sense in which we have so far used the term *standardisation*, no spoken language can ever be fully standardised. If we return to Saussure's famous analogy of the game of chess and use the analogy in a different way, we can compare language use to a game of chess in which different people may occasionally play the game by different rules. In chess, it would clearly be inconvenient and irritating if one player moved his pawns diagonally instead of vertically, and even more inconvenient if, in the course of time, one player unilaterally and silently changed his own rules of play in some particular ways. This is what does happen in language use. Different people and different communities play to some extent by different rules and the rules change (silently) in the course of time. As a result of this, miscommunications can occur.

Cross-dialectal miscomprehension and miscommunication have not been investigated to any extent, and text-books are often content to state that Standard English is the variety most accessible to the majority of people and leave it at that. While it is clear that active use of spoken English varies considerably, our own researches (J. Milroy, 1978 and 1981; L. Milroy, 1984), also lead us to believe that passive *comprehension* of Standard English is by no means as uniform or absolute as it might appear. Conversely, as Labov (1972c) has demonstrated, the accessibility of non-standard forms to Standard English speakers is even less certain. Speakers of one variety (whether it is called the standard or not) do not necessarily have intuitions about all aspects of the grammar of other varieties, and so there are constructions that they do not immediately understand.

Some examples of cross-dialectal miscomprehension in syntax have already been discussed in print (J. Milroy, 1978; L. Milroy, 1984; J. Harris, 1982). They can easily be added to, and we shall enumerate some relevant non-standard usages in Chapter 4. For the moment, we again notice as an example the categorical distinction between the singular and plural 2nd person pronoun (see above p. 14), which is found mainly in Scottish and Irish varieties of English.

The following quotation is from tape-recordings made during fieldwork in Belfast:

So I said to our Trish and our Sandra: 'Yous wash the dishes'. I might as well have said: 'You wash the dishes', for our Trish just got up and put her coat on and went out.

Not only does this speaker demonstrate that she has in her pronoun system a categorical distinction here between *you* and *yous*, she also assumes (wrongly) that the fieldworker has the same distinction. There were many cases both in the fieldwork and in daily life where miscomprehension was evident. Often, when a group of people was addressed as *you* (SE plural), individuals would look round to see which single member of the group was being addressed. Instances such as this may seem small in themselves, but the problem is that we cannot know how often such miscomprehensions go *unrepaired*. *Yous*-dialect users might be rather offended by a person who leaves a conversational group with the comment *I'll see you tomorrow*, each of them believing that he has addressed a certain member of the group and deliberately snubbed the others.

There is also a (possibly apocryphal) story about a Yorkshire car-driver who was run over by a train because he interpreted the word *while* to mean 'until' (as it does in Yorkshire) at a level crossing where the sign said 'Wait while the red light flashes'. Such disastrous consequences are no doubt rare; yet miscomprehensions that arise from cross-dialectal differences can certainly lead to bafflement and even resentment. It is important to recognise that they occur, and also necessary to recognise that those most likely to suffer as a result are non-standard speakers. People are assumed to have full passive competence in the standard, but standard speakers do not normally learn the differing rules of non-standard varieties. Moreover, such difficulties occur not only in ordinary conversational contact, but also in formal contexts such as class-rooms, where a middle-class teacher's unfamiliarity with the vern-acular usage of a pupil could also lead to misunderstanding and unnecessary difficulty (see Trudgill, 1975:48 for an example).

One reason why possible cross-dialectal miscomprehensions have not been much investigated is that non-standard norms of usage have usually been ignored, or considered careless and ignorant deviations from 'grammar' when they have been noticed. Language guardians always consider non-standard usage (and sometimes standard colloquialisms) to arise from the perversity of speakers or from cognitive deficiency (an inability to learn what is 'correct'). In addition, at least one influential branch of linguistics has tended to discourage systematic observation of actual usage. In the 1960s, Chomsky argued against 'corpus-based' linguistics. As a result, much of the grammatical theorising of the 1960s and 1970s was based on the middle-class Standard English of the scholars themselves (for a critique of this see Labov, 1972b:292). It was further assumed that differences between dialects were probably only superficial (we shall see in Chapter 4 that there are at least some dialectal differences that are very deep-rooted). It seems to us that those who proposed and accepted these theories may them-selves have been influenced by the ideology of standardisation, which inclines us all to view a language as a relatively fixed, in-variant and unchanging entity. Far from advocating the teaching of non-standard dialects in schools (as Honey, 1983, apparently believes), the Chomskyan tradition has been implicitly pro-standard and possibly even prescriptive in some of its effects.

Although we have referred loosely to 'Standard English', there is – in the very strict sense in which we have so far used the term 'standardisation' – no such entity as a standard spoken language; even so-called 'Standard English' can be perceived to incorporate variability and change. On the phonological level, for instance, the 'Received Pronunciation' of Standard English appears to permit some variation, e.g. between 'long' and 'short' /u/ and /ʊ/ (as in RP *food* and *foot*) in forms like *room* and *toothbrush*. Examples from all levels of language can easily be multiplied. Standardis-ation, as Swift perceived, prevents or inhibits change and variation, and the ideology of standardisation is inimical to change and vari-ation. Therefore, a label like 'Standard English' is a rather loose and pre-scientific label. What Standard English actually is thought to be depends on acceptance (mainly by the most influential people) of a common core of linguistic conventions, and a good deal of fuz-ziness remains around the edges. The ideology of standardisation, whatever merits there may be in it, tends to blind us to the some-what ill-defined nature of a standard language, and may have some undesirable consequences in that it leads to over-simplified views of the nature of language, evidently held even by highly educated speakers.

The term *standardisation*, which we have defined strictly, has been used by certain scholars (e.g. Haugen, 1972) in a somewhat looser sense. Its chief characteristic, according to our account, is intolerance of optional variability in language. In the view of others, this perception is allied to a number of other stages of 'standardisation' that appear to have been involved in the histories of languages (on which see 2.1 for an account of the development of Standard English). According to these scholars, a standard language is one which has minimal variation of form and maximal variation of function (Leith, 1983:32). Such a definition is a suitably relative one, but it is clear that the various stages that are usually involved in the development of a standard language may be described as the consequence of a need for uniformity that is felt by influential portions of society at a given time. A variety is then *selected* as a standard (competing varieties might no doubt be selected by different parts of the community, yet only one of them might become the standard in the long run); this variety is now *accepted* by influential people, and then *diffused* geographically and socially by various means (official papers, the educational system, the writing system, discrimination of various kinds, both direct and indirect, against non-standard speakers). Thus some scholars (Giles *et al*, 1974, 1975; Leith, 1983) speak of the standard as an imposed, or superposed, variety. Once it is well established and has defeated its competitors, the standard language must then be *maintained*. Maintenance comes about through various means. As a result of *elaboration of function*, the standard is perceived by those who are socially mobile to be of more value than other varieties for purely utilitarian ends. It also acquires *prestige*, as it is noticed that the most successful people use it in writing and, to a great extent, in speech. It is also maintained through the inculcation of literacy, as the writing system is then held up as the model of 'correctness' (see below). Thus, the writing system serves as one of the sources of prescriptive norms, and *prescription* becomes more intense after the language undergoes *codification* (as in eighteenth century England), because speakers then have access to dictionaries and grammar-books, which they regard as authorities. They tend to believe that the 'language' is enshrined in these books (however many mistakes and omissions there may be in them) rather than in the linguistic and communicative competence of the millions who use the language every day.

The account we have given of these stages in the standardisation process is not precisely the same as that given by others, and the reader should note that these hypothetical stages do not necessarily follow one another in temporal succession. Some stages may overlap with others, and the stage we have described as *maintenance* starts quite early in the process and then continues throughout. We prefer to consider these stages as stages of *implementation* of the standard rather than as aspects of standardisation itself. The process of standardisation (strictly defined) is based on the idea of aiming, by any means possible, at uniformity. These additional stages are stages that have been observed to follow from the ideology of standardisation, which in the case of English was explicitly espoused by Caxton as long ago as 1490. However this may be, the ideology of the standard is still with us, and we pass on in the next chapter to discuss some of the ways in which the process of maintaining the idea of a standard is implemented at the present day.

2

Standard English and the complaint tradition

2.1 The history of Standard English

Most people are of the opinion that the influence of the mass media in recent times has had a powerful effect in reducing the diversity of English and bringing about uniformity. This is not a proven fact: it is merely a belief. In favour of this view, it can be reasonably argued that remote rural dialects have been dying out quite rapidly. Against it, we can point out that although the Received ·Pronunciation of Standard English has been heard constantly on radio and then television for over 60 years, only 3 to 5% of the population of Britain actually speak RP (Trudgill and Hannah, 1982). It can also be pointed out that the spread of English to former colonies has continued to create diversity, and new brands of English have been springing up even in recent times (on Singaporean English, see Chapter 5).

There are three areas of research that suggest that the promotion of standardisation through official and centralised channels is less widely effective than is generally believed. One is the study of variation in English in the British Isles. The phonological structure (pronunciation) of regional forms of English does not appear to adapt rapidly towards the standard. For example Belfast English (as described by J. Milroy, 1981) has a radically different phonological system from that of SE, and that system remains different in spite of radio, television and the educational system. Belfast English (and other Hiberno-English) pronunciation preserves certain structural characteristics of Early Modern English that have long been lost in SE (Milroy and Harris, 1980): these varieties and many others, although they change quite rapidly in some ways, have successfully resisted centralising influences for centuries. A second relevant area is research into the language of the mass media themselves. For example, Bell (1982), in a study of the language of several New Zealand radio channels, has shown that broadcasters tend to adapt to the language of their target audiences, following rather than leading in language variation and change. A third relevant area (one that has not been noticed so far by linguistic researchers) is the general study of diffusion of innovations in society (Rogers and Shoemaker, 1971, and see Milroy and Milroy, forthcoming).

The general concern of this tradition of research is with the manner in which innovations of any kind – for example, in fashion, speech or technology – eventually become widely adopted by a population. Rogers and Shoemaker note that a number of very general principles can be discerned in the process of diffusion and adoption, and the finding which is of relevance here is that *personal* channels of communication are very much more influential than *mass media* channels in persuading persons to adopt innovations. Generally, mass media channels effectively give rise to *awareness* of an innovation, but have little influence in promoting *adoption*. There is no reason to think that the diffusion of linguistic innovations will follow principles different from those governing the diffusion of other kinds of innovation. Indeed, it seems to be the case that the media have successfully promoted an awareness of the standard spoken language (which is in fact popularly known as BBC English) without having much influence on the rate of adoption of that standard. As we shall see, a number of factors relating to the individual speaker's everyday social contacts seem, as diffusion theory would predict, to be the major influences on the language behaviour of the individual speaker.

There is therefore little evidence to support the popular view that mass communications inevitably bring about uniformity of usage; yet we can say that standardisation has advanced over the centuries *in certain ways*. First, there is no doubt that great uniformity has been achieved in the *written* channel: the scribe of *Havelok the Dane* (c. 1300) used a writing system that permitted many variations in spelling: the word *right*, for example, could be spelt as *riht*, *rith*, *richt*, *ricth*, *rist*. Twentieth-century spelling, on the other hand, permits virtually no variation. The second sense in which standardisation may be said to have advanced is in the promotion of a standard ideology, i.e. a public *consciousness* of the standard. People *believe* that there is a 'right' way of using English, although they do not necessarily use the 'correct' forms in their own speech.

Thus, although radio, film and television may not have had much influence on everyday speech, they are amongst the many influences that promote a consciousness of the standard and maintain its position.

In these special senses, the standardisation of English has been in progress for many centuries. The process of linguistic normalisation can be traced in the gradual progression towards greater uniformity in *written* English. Similarly, the *elaboration of function* that is associated with standardisation can be traced in the spread of English into all areas of life: in the Middle Ages after the Norman Conquest, English was seldom used in legal or administrative functions (Norman French being the 'official' language), and Latin rather than English remained the language of learning to a great extent even as late as the seventeenth century. In 1545 the physician Thomas Phaire had to apologise for writing in English and complained (Neale and Wallis, eds 1957:13):

> why grutche they phisyke to come forth in Englyshe? Woulde they have no man to know but onely they?
> ('Why are they reluctant to allow medical knowledge to be made public in English? Do they want no one but themselves to know?')

Complaints like that of Phaire reflect consciousness of the need for the native language to be used in a greater variety of functions, and elaboration of function necessarily involves elaboration of vocabulary. We shall see that one aspect of the 'linguistic complaint' tradition is directly concerned with this elaborated vocabulary (see 2.3 below).

In this chapter we are concerned with the progressive standardisation of English, but in particular with the way in which the standard ideology has been, and is being, promoted and maintained. One useful way of charting the history of standardisation is to look at the history of linguistic *complaint* from the Middle Ages onward, and to relate this to present-day continuations of the complaint tradition.

Medieval complaints about language were not usually of the kind that have become most familiar since about 1700, i.e. complaints about supposed incorrect usage; they were more concerned with the relative status of French and English in the Kingdom. They therefore reflect the gradual rise in the status of English and, indirectly, the movement towards elaboration in the functions of

English. Already in the early fourteenth century it is clear that French is no longer in general use, although it is officially required. In 1327, for example, Ranulph Higden complains that English is being corrupted by French and attributes this corruption to the fact that schoolchildren are forced to abandon their own language and construe their lessons in French. By the middle of the century, however, lessons were being taught in English. John Trevisa (the translator of Higden's '*Polychronicon*') observes that this has advantages and disadvantages, the main disadvantage being that children now know no more French than does 'their left heel'. He also remarks that even gentlemen 'haueþ now moche i-left for to teche here children Frensche' ('have now largely abandoned teaching their children French').

These comments are symptoms of the movement towards establishing English, rather than French, as the official language of England. This official status was recognised to an extent by the Statute of Pleading in 1362, which made English a language of the lawcourts (for a discussion of the fourteenth-century language situation see Baugh and Cable, 1978:143–50).

After the demise of French, the social history of English can be described as a long and gradual struggle to acquire greater respectability and a wide range of official, public and academic functions, not merely as the language of administration and law, but also as the language of printed books and of science, medicine, theology and philosophy. This struggle to acquire more functions involved progressive *elaboration* of vocabulary, and is reflected in the complaints of many writers. The struggle to promote *uniformity* in written usage can also be traced in the complaint tradition.

The most important early complaint about the form of English (as distinct from its status and functions) is that of William Caxton (1490), the earliest English printer. Caxton complained that the language was too variable, and that people from different places could hardly understand one another. He was quite clearly implying that standardisation in the strict sense (lack of variation in form) was needed.

And certaynly our langage now vsed varyeth ferre from that whiche was vsed and spoken whan I was borne. For we englysshe men ben borne vnder the domynacyon of the mone, whiche is neuer stedfaste, but euer wauerynge, wexynge one season, and waneth & dycreaseth another season. And that comyn englysshe that is spoken in one shyre varyeth from a nother...certaynly it is harde to playse euery man by cause of dyuersite & chaunge of langage. (Bolton, 1966:2–3)

Caxton, as a publisher, had pressing practical reasons for desiring a standard written form of the language. He solved his problem by using as the literary standard a variety based on the South-East Midland area, but his selection was not made on strictly linguistic grounds. The variety he decided to use had already achieved some prominence – but not necessarily because it was the most expressive or the most beautiful. It was the obvious choice because the area concerned was the most prominent politically, commercially and academically. This variety is the basis of modern Standard English. If the North-West of England had been the most influential area, Standard English would be a descendant of the dialect of *Sir Gawain and the Green Knight* (a long, courtly poem in the Arthurian tradition), and it would be a very different form of Standard English from what we actually have today. All the dialects of English were in principle equally good candidates (on linguistic grounds) for standardisation, but from the fifteenth century onwards the SE Midland variety was superimposed on the others as a standard (for a discussion see Leith, 1983:32–57).

Complaints about English in the sixteenth century usually focus on its supposed inadequacies when compared with Latin and Greek and even with other more fashionable non-classical languages such as French and Italian. They are associated with the rise to prominence of English as a 'standard' language in so far as they reflect the feeling that English needed a wider vocabulary. Often, the writers complain in terms of the lack of 'eloquence' of English, but underlying these complaints are the political and commercial pressures that made it necessary for the language to have an elaborated vocabulary.

Complaints about specific aspects of English usage (e.g. use of prepositions and fine distinctions between meanings of different words) do not commonly occur until the position of English as the official language (in almost all its functions) was virtually assured – around 1700. The great classic of complaint literature is Swift's (1712) 'Proposal for Correcting, Improving and Ascertaining the English Tongue', which, after a polite preamble, begins as follows:

My Lord, I do here, in the name of all the learned and Polite Persons of the Nation, complain to Your Lordship as *First*

Minister, that our Language is extremely imperfect; that its daily
Improvements are by no means in proportion to its daily Corrup-
fions; that the Pretenders to polish and refine it, have chiefly
multiplied Abuses and Absurdities; and, that in many Instances,
it offends against every Part of Grammar. (Bolton, 1966:108)

These sentiments expressed here remain familiar at the present day.
Indeed the contents of Swift's 'Proposal' anticipate, in principle,
almost every attitude expressed in modern complaint literature (on
which see below).

Swift recommended that an official body (similar to the
Academies of France and Italy) should be set up, first to improve
the language, and second, to 'ascertain' (we might now say 'standardise') it. He said that he could see no reason why language
should be perpetually changing and believed that English had
perceptibly declined since the Restoration (in 1660). As usual in
complaint literature, someone or something had to be blamed for
this supposed decline. Today it is often the teaching profession or
politicians (Orwell, 1946), and sometimes, as we have seen, the
scapegoat is now the discipline of linguistics itself (Simon, 1980;
Honey, 1983). Swift blamed the loose morals of the post-
Restoration period – 'University boys' and frequenters of coffee-
houses. However, in his argument he made it clear that he regarded
the basic problem to be the fact of variation and change in
language: in his complaint he was, amongst other things, reflecting
the need of a developing nation and colonial power to have a
relatively fixed standard language for the practical purpose of clear
communication over long distances and periods of time (chiefly in
writing, but also presumably in speech).

It is well known that in linguistic matters, the eighteenth century
was largely, but not wholly, a century of authoritarianism and
prescription. During that century much of the necessary work of
codifying the standard language was carried out, notably in Dr
Johnson's *Dictionary* (1755) and in a spate of grammar books by
such men as Bishop Lowth (1762) and Lindley Murray (1795). The
task of Swift's proposed academy was in fact carried out informally by private persons. The tone of most of this work was legis-
lative, setting out how the language ought to be used, not necessarily
how it actually *was* used by the majority of people. To that period
we owe many of the school grammar prescriptions that are current
today, such as the ban on double (or multiple) negatives, and the
preference for 'different *from*' and 'It is *I*'.

It is difficult to assess how successful the eighteenth-century legislators were in achieving their aim of suppressing variation in language. They seem to have been successful in codifying a set of conventions appropriate for the written language – conventions which have not changed greatly since that time. The orthography, for example, has changed very little since Dr Johnson codified the spelling in his dictionary. Clearly, they were answering the need of a developing nation for reliable communication in writing, and in this they have been generally successful.

They have had much less success in preventing change in the *spoken* language. The economic and social upheavals of the nineteenth century resulted in the rise of large industrial cities whose distinctive dialects now differ from the rural areas around them and also from high prestige English; many millions of speakers use them. As a result, multiple negatives and hundreds of other 'nonstandard' features continue to enjoy a flourishing life. Even in the eighteenth century, the greatest English language scholar of the time finally came to realise the futility of attempting to prevent all change. After his labours on the dictionary (which was at first intended to prescribe and standardise usage), Dr Johnson had this to say:

> with...justice may the lexicographer be derided, who...shall imagine that his dictionary can embalm his language...
>
> With this hope, however, academies have been instituted, to guard the avenues of their languages, to retain fugitives, and repulse intruders; but their vigilance and activity have hitherto been vain; sounds are too volatile and subtle for legal restraints; to enchain syllables, and to lash the wind, are equally the undertakings of pride, unwilling to measure its desires by its strength.
> (Bolton, 1966: 151–2)

Modern inheritors of the prescriptive tradition would do well to emulate this wisdom and humility, acquired as it had been from extensive language scholarship over many years. As we shall see, they seldom do, and they seldom have adequate knowledge of the nature of language.

The achievement of the eighteenth century has sometimes been disparaged. Some modern scholars have been hostile to that achievement and have been very scathing about the 'traditional grammar' and 'notions of correctness' that derive from that century. While it is true that the language has continued to change despite the legislators of that century, and while it is also true that many of their prescriptions (e.g. *it is I* rather than *it's me*) are absurd when applied to speech, the eighteenth century was a successful culmination of a long process. Its achievement was to establish, through codification, a much more widespread consciousness of a relatively uniform 'correct' English than had been possible before. Advances in technology and means of communication were at the same time spreading the written word much more widely than ever before. Subsequent advances in literacy and in mass education have continued to ensure that the public has looked to the relatively standardised written channel as the model of correctness, despite the fact that spoken English has continued to change. What the eighteenth century finally established was what we have called the *ideology of standardisation*, to which virtually every speaker now subscribes in principle.

In Chapter 3 we shall go on to consider in more detail the nature of language change and the opposing mechanisms of language maintenance (including codification of the kind achieved in the eighteenth century). In the remainder of this chapter we focus on twentieth-century continuations of the complaint tradition.

2.2   The function of language complaints in maintaining the standard

We have suggested that the chief linguistic characteristic of standardisation is suppression of optional variation at all levels of language – in pronunciation (phonology), spelling, grammar (morphology and syntax) and lexicon. Standardisation is therefore partly aimed at preventing or inhibiting linguistic change (Swift, 1712). It is clear that the movement towards a national standard language in England arose not primarily because authoritarian individuals wished to impose complete conformity on everyone else, but in response to wider social, political and commercial needs. Caxton needed a standard language for printed books, and eighteenth-century authoritarianism was a symptom of the requirements of British society at that time. Standardisation, particularly in the written channel, was needed for reasons of efficient communication over long distances and periods of time.

The standard ideology is promoted through public channels: in the past, standardisation has first affected the writing system, and literacy has subsequently become the main influence in promoting the consciousness of the standard ideology. The norms of written and formal English have then been codified in dictionaries, grammars and handbooks of usage and inculcated by prescription through the educational system. Standardisation through prescription has clearly been most successful in the written channel: in the daily conversation of ordinary speakers, however, it has been less effective. Indeed, the norms of colloquial, as against formal, English have not been codified to any extent.

The effect of codification and prescription has been to *legitimise* the norms of formal registers of standard English rather than the norms of everyday spoken English. Codifiers have legislated and prescribers have tried to put the legislation into effect. One result of this is that there is a general belief that there is only one form of correct, i.e. legitimate, English, and a feeling that colloquial and non-standard forms are perverse and deliberate deviations from what is approved by 'law'; i.e. they are 'illegitimate'.

Outside the schoolroom, the standard ideology has been most openly promoted by writers in what we have called 'the complaint tradition'. This tradition can, however, be divided into two broad types. It is most important that the characteristics of these types should be clearly distinguished, as a failure to recognise their different aims can result in vagueness and confusion in popular commentaries on language use (see for example 2.5 below).

Type 1 complaints, which are implicitly legalistic and which are concerned with correctness, attack 'misuse' of specific parts of the phonology, grammar, vocabulary of English (and in the case of written English 'errors' of spelling, punctuation, etc.). Type 2 complaints, which we may call 'moralistic', recommend clarity in writing and attack what appear to be abuses of language that may mislead and confuse the public. The elements of Type 1 complaints are fully anticipated in Swift's proposal of 1712, except that Swift argued his case more fully and skilfully than any twentieth-century Type 1 complaints that we have seen (he specified quite clearly that he was promoting standardisation), and some elements of Type 2 complaints are also anticipated by Swift. The correctness tradition (Type 1) is wholly dedicated to the maintenance of the norms of standard English in preference to other varieties: sometimes writers in this tradition attempt to justify the usages they favour and condemn those they dislike by appeals to logic, etymology and so forth. Very often, however, they make no attempt whatever to explain why one usage is correct and another incorrect: they simply take it for granted that the proscribed form is *obviously* unacceptable and illegitimate; in short, they believe in a transcendental norm of correct English.

Type 2 complaints do not devote themselves to stigmatising specific errors in grammar, phonology, and so on. They accept the fact of standardisation in the written channel, and they are concerned with clarity, effectiveness, morality and honesty in the public use of the standard language. Sometimes elements of Type 1 can enter into Type 2 complaints, in that the writers may sometimes condemn non-standard usage in the belief that it is careless or in some way reprehensible; yet the two types of complaint can in general be sharply distinguished. The most important modern author in this second tradition is George Orwell, and we shall consider his views in 2.4; in the remainder of this section, we consider the tradition of 'correctness'.

Type 1 complaints (on correctness) may be directed against 'errors' in either spoken or written language, and they frequently do not make a very clear distinction between the two. Simon (1980), for example, complains about misuse of apostrophes – as in *wing's* (plural) for *wings* – but also about spoken usage, such as *you was* for *you were*. He lumps all these 'faults' together as 'illiteracies', clearly assuming that the model for spoken language lies in the written channel, and believing that all reasonable readers will agree with him. The structure and function of spoken language, however, is altogether different from that of written language (see below, Chapter 3.2, 3.3).

From vast numbers of letters to newspapers, we may quote the following complaint about spoken usage as typical:

> For many years I have been disgusted with the bad grammar used by school-leavers and teachers too sometimes, but recently on the lunch-time news, when a secretary, who had just started work with a firm, was interviewed her first words were: 'I looked up and seen two men' etc. It's unbelievable to think, with so many young people out of work, that she could get such a job, but perhaps 'I seen' and 'I done' etc., is the usual grammar nowadays for office staff and business training colleges. ('Have Went'; Saintfield, N. Ireland).

This correspondent no doubt sees himself or herself as a guardian of 'correctness', and the letter is clearly predicated on the assumption that if people want to get decent jobs they ought to speak correctly (just as they should have good table manners). It is implied that the secretary who says *seen* for *saw* may be keeping better people (who speak correctly) out of jobs, and the remark that '"I seen" and "I done" etc.' may be the 'usual grammar nowadays' carries with it the implication that at some time in the past standards of language use were better than they are now. The idea of linguistic decline is always either directly addressed or hinted at in the correctness tradition. Furthermore, the idea of linguistic decline usually carries with it the implication that general standards of conduct and morality in society are also in decline. The clearest statement of this view, as we have noted, is contained in Swift's 'Proposal', but see also the remarks of Rae (1982) quoted in 2.5.

It is unlikely that 'Have Went' fully understands the social function that he or she is carrying out. The letter is one of thousands of similar contributions to the maintenance of a standard language, and discrimination against those who do not use it in speech. Nor is the correspondent aware that attempts to maintain a single *spoken* standard have not been very successful. The choice of *saw* as the 'correct' form is ultimately arbitrary, and despite the efforts of the complaint tradition, many millions of people persist in their daily conversation in using non-standard grammatical forms, e.g.

- 'You was there, wasn't you?'
- 'I never said nothing.'
- 'Them houses is nice.'
- 'It were a right mess.'
- 'That's the man what I saw yesterday.'

The arbitrariness of some of these judgements must at this point be noticed again. Expressions like *you was* appear to have been fashionable in polite society in the late seventeenth and eighteenth centuries (Wyld, 1936); 19th century novelists represent well-educated characters as using *he don't*; in earlier times the *for-to* complement, as in *he went down the road for to see his mother* was normal in literary English (e.g. in Chaucer and Caxton). Shakespeare and his contemporaries used double negatives in their writing and often failed to distinguish between past tense and past participle forms, as in

'I have already *chose* my officer.' (*Othello*, I, 1)

In pronunciation, it appears that the present-day substitution of [ɪn] for [ɪŋ], as in *huntin'* for *hunting*, has a long and complicated history that suggests that the [ɪn] form is closer to the 'original': it is also well known that upper-class speakers in living memory stereotypically used such expressions as *huntin'*, *shootin' and fishin'*. One of the most stigmatised forms of all − [h]-dropping − also appears (as we have seen) to have a long history (J. Milroy, 1983), and it may also have been fashionable in middle-class and/or polite society in Elizabethan times and before. Thus usages that are favoured at one time may be stigmatised at another for reasons that have nothing to do with linguistic values, but which are purely social.

Complaints about non-standard usage, however, continue to appear in very large numbers in newspapers and journals. Sometimes full-length books appear that promote the use of 'correct' English and criticise the supposed decline of the language (although such books normally contain or imply elements of both types of complaint). The writers concerned range all the way from ordinary newspaper readers to prominent journalists and established literary men and women. To the extent that such complaints are of Type 1, they universally share the assumptions of 'Have Went, Saintfield'. These may be summarised as follows:

1. That there is one, and only one, correct way of speaking and/or writing the English language.
2. That deviations from this norm are illiteracies, or barbarisms, and that non-standard forms are irregular and perversely deviant.
3. That people *ought* to use the standard language and that it is quite right to discriminate against non-standard users, as such usage is a sign of stupidity, ignorance, perversity, moral degeneracy, etc.

Thus, while Type 1 complaints appear to be attacks on detailed points of *usage*, they are actually making claims about the superiority of one language *system* over another (without usually being explicit about this, and often being apparently unaware of it). The assumption is that a particular abstract set of linguistic rules (in phonology, spelling, grammar and lexicon) is inherently superior to some other abstract set. In this way, Type 1 complaints must be sharply distinguished from the 'moralistic' complaints of Type 2. The latter do not focus on non-standard deviations from standard norms, but are concerned with the *usage* of *standard* English in public, formal and written channels, and the effects of such usage on society and human behaviour.

2.3 Correctness and semantic shift

Complaints about correctness of the kind represented by Simon (1980) and 'Have Went' are extremely common, and they extend back for centuries. Although there is little change in the substance of the complaints, they seem to have had little or no effect on usage. No matter how often the writers complain about 'you was' and the misuse of apostrophes, millions of people cheerfully continue to use the proscribed forms, and dialects that differ from the standard language continue to flourish.

Type 2 complaints, as we have pointed out, differ radically from these, as they are generally concerned with public usage in written and formal styles: they attempt to encourage clarity, precision and effectiveness in the use of *standard* English. Sometimes, however, it is difficult to classify a particular complaint as belonging clearly to one of these two types. Complaints about careless usage of written *vocabulary* are very common, and they can often be said to contain characteristics of both types. In so far as they oppose the tendency of language to change, they are of Type 1; in so far as they are concerned with careful and effective written usage, they are of Type 2.

A well-reasoned example of this mixed type is an essay by Kingsley Amis (1980) entitled 'Getting it wrong'. Amis is concerned primarily with lexical confusion (malapropism), but also with slightly vague or 'incorrect' usage of words. His many examples are drawn from the written work of professional journalists and authors, who might well be expected 'to know better'.

Malapropisms arise from accidental phonetic similarities between words of different meanings, and Amis's examples include many common 'mistakes', such as confusion of *flout*: 'express contempt for' with *flaunt*: 'wave, show off', as in

> It flaunts (i.e. flouts) every rational calculation of British currency.

Other examples are *mitigate* for 'militate' and *perpetrate* for 'perpetuate'. Amis also cites examples, however, that are not so much malapropisms as slight semantic shifts: the words concerned are used, not in completely unrelated meanings (as in malapropisms), but in slightly shifted meanings that are considered to be incorrect. An example of this is the use of *crescendo* ('a noise that rises from soft to loud') to mean 'a loud noise', thus an expression such as 'the sound rose to a crescendo' is considered to be incorrect.

Malapropisms do not usually lead to permanent change of meaning (although it must be admitted that *flaunt* for *flout* is at present a strong candidate), but slight semantic shifts of a logically motivated kind are the very stuff of semantic change. Such shifts lead in the first place to *polysemy* (the development of more than one meaning), and in the course of time the etymological meaning may be forgotten, as transferred but related meanings take over. For Milton, *obvious* meant 'in the way' (Latin, *ob*: 'against'; *via*: 'way'), and 'the extravagant and erring spirit' of Shakespeare's *Hamlet* did not spend lavishly or make mistakes: *extravagant* and *erring* had their etymological meanings: 'straying outside' and 'wandering'. There must have been some time in the past when the literal meanings of these words co-existed with the present-day transferred or figurative meanings.

In cases like *crescendo*, and in the common use of *aggravate* to mean 'annoy', we are witnessing the same process. In musical terminology, *crescendo* will continue to be used in its precise technical sense, while the average speaker will continue to 'misuse' it, but in a closely associated meaning. In effect, this word, with thousands of others, has developed two related meanings, and statements by the guardians will not prevent or reverse such changes. Semantic change is a universal process.

It is possible, however, that the English language has been in recent centuries particularly prone to rapid semantic change for the reason that it has annexed a vast elaborated vocabulary that is not native to English. This vocabulary (which includes *crescendo*, *perpetuate*, *mitigate* and so forth) is literary, formal or technical: the average speaker makes use of it much less often than writers do, and access to this vocabulary is difficult for those who do not have extensive classical and humanistic education. It is to be expected that, as these words pass from formal and literary usage into occasional use in speech, their meanings will drift. Thus the elaborated vocabulary that is associated with standardisation may itself be a liability in so far as it provides a focus for semantic shift − a tendency that standardisation attempts to suppress.

Professional writers usually prefer to fight a rearguard action on semantic change, and it is worth enquiring why this is so and whether it should be so. We may attempt to answer the first question by pointing to the differences that naturally exist between the functions of written language and those of conversational speech, and the tensions set up by these differences. For various reasons, written language (especially prose) has to be more careful and precise than spoken; the effects of ambiguity and vagueness are more difficult to overcome in writing than in speech: miscomprehension of a written text (arising from careless writing) cannot be repaired, as the writer is not present to explain 'what he really meant' when the text is being read. Uncontrolled semantic change can therefore be dysfunctional for writers. If words change in meaning too rapidly, their writings could be misunderstood at some later date.

As written texts can survive over long periods, professional writers often interpret the forces of linguistic change as inimical to their own interests. One of Swift's (1712) motives for proposing 'ascertainment' of the language was to make sure that eighteenth-century writing would be comprehensible to future generations. Alexander Pope pointed to the language of Chaucer, which, after only three centuries, had become difficult to read; he lamented,

'For such as Chaucer is shall Dryden be'.

The same general motive seems to underlie the efforts of present day authors: they may feel it to be in their own interests (and the general interest) to promote the standard ideology, as this tends to ensure reliability in the use of what we have called 'the counters in the system' (1.5), and therefore maintains some control over language change.

Yet, although professional writers have usually spoken in favour of fixed and stable linguistic forms, there is one sense in which it might not be appropriate for them to do so. It is not professional writers, but lawyers, administrators and scientists, who require the most rigid forms of standardisation. A legal document (unlike a novel or poem) must be drawn up in such a way that it cannot be subject to varying interpretations, and the terms used must have precise meanings. Similarly, technical terminology in scientific disciplines must be precise. One might therefore expect imaginative writers to wish to exploit flexibility and variation in language, rather than upholding narrow versions of the standard ideology. Some innovative writers have in fact done this; yet it was a poet and critic who uttered this strong statement on the fixed meanings of words: 'Words...represent concepts...(they communicate) by virtue of their conceptual identity, and in so far as this identity is impaired, they will communicate with less force and precision' (Winters, 1966: 37–8).

The professional writer's position in this matter is a difficult one. In upholding the standard ideology, he is acting partly in his own interests, but mainly in what he interprets as the general interest. It is in the interests of society that written and formal communication should be as precise and unambiguous as possible, but not perhaps wholly in the interests of imaginative writers. If literary people expound views on language that are narrow, pedantic and unrealistic, they may have the effect of inhibiting innovation and creativity in imaginative writing. One author who clearly understood the social functions of the written channel was George Orwell: we shall consider his work in the next section.

2.4   George Orwell and the moralistic tradition

Orwell was a moralist, and in linguistic matters he was to a great extent also a realist. Most of his work contains occasional comments that amount to criticism of language use — usually criticism of centralised and bureaucratic language. His best-known criticisms, however, are embodied in the essay 'Politics and the English Language' and in the invented language 'Newspeak' in the novel *Nineteen Eighty-Four*. But in a lesser-known essay, 'Propaganda and Demotic Speech' (1944), Orwell makes it clear that he understands more about language use than most of those who complain about usage.

Orwell's complaints focus on the distance between centralised, bureaucratic language and the 'real' usage of ordinary people. Unlike writers in the correctness tradition, he represents a position that is *against* some aspects of the standard ideology (at least in so far as it is manifested in formal styles) and *in favour of* 'demotic speech'. He mentions the stilted bookish language (cf. the elaborated vocabulary that we discussed above) and upper class accents of the news bulletins, and comments that this language is totally ineffective in communicating with the ordinary public. He attacks the artificiality and emptiness of propaganda slogans and political jargon — *objectively, counter-revolutionary, left-deviationism* and the like. Orwell is concerned with failures in communication and with the appropriacy of language styles to their purposes. In the 1944 essay, his most important general point is that there is a huge gap between written and spoken language. Few, if any, of the language complaint writers have recognised this clearly, possibly because their interests have been narrower than those of Orwell; they have not taken as much interest in the multiple *social* functions of language.

'The main weakness of propagandists and popularizers', says Orwell, 'is their failure to notice that spoken and written language are two different things.' Lecturers use elaborated clause structures that may be appropriate to formal written language, but which are not appropriate in speech because they are difficult to comprehend. Broadcasters use words that are literary in nature: the vocabulary of English, he says, contains thousands of words used in writing that have 'no real currency' in speech (they are in fact drawn from the elaborated vocabulary of standard literary English). As he is largely concerned with broadcast language, he then goes on to recommend ways of making it sound more like spoken English. 'To get genuine spoken English on to paper is a complicated matter.' Unlike most of the complaint writers, Orwell then goes on to make positive proposals for improvement.

When in 'Politics and the English Language', Orwell says that 'the English language is in a bad way', it is not therefore ordinary English speech that he is criticising. As the rest of the essay makes quite clear, he is disturbed by the dead metaphors (of politicians and other public figures) that are 'tacked together like the sections of a prefabricated henhouse': his own excellent writing actually shows that the language *as a whole* is more than serviceable, and not in 'a bad way'. Orwell's concern here, and in the 'language' 'Newspeak' of *Nineteen Eighty-Four*, is with the idea that 'misuse' of language can corrupt thought. Euphemistic jargon can 'make murder respectable and give the appearance of solidity to pure wind'.

Orwell's ideas are of the greatest interest to those who are concerned with the nature of authority in language and with language prescription. The linguistic abuses that he is criticising are not primarily found in the colloquial speech of ordinary people: they are found in centralised and official speeches and documents, and they are uttered or written in 'standard English'. He is criticising authority in language and some aspects of language use that are consequences of standardisation.

However forceful and original his views may seem to be, Orwell's work can be seen as related to at least two other traditions in language study. One is the 'Pure English' tradition, which surfaced in the sixteenth century and then reappeared in a stronger

form in the nineteenth. The other is a view of language associated
with the work of Benjamin Lee Whorf and Edward Sapir. In its
strongest form, the Sapir-Whorf hypothesis proposes that our
thought processes are conditioned by the structure of the language
we speak. In his parable of the future, Orwell envisages an
authoritarian state in which the expressive and intellectual content
of language has been reduced to nothing, and in which users of the
language are denied access to critical and abstract thought by the
limitations deliberately imposed on that language. It would be an
exaggeration to say that Newspeak is the ultimate in language *standardisation*, but it is the ultimate in centrally planned and imposed
use of language.

'Official' language is characterised by a relatively high proportion of words borrowed from Latin and Greek; as Orwell certainly
perceived, and as we have noted above, access to this elaborated
vocabulary is not particularly easy for the ordinary person. While
explorations of the resources of this vocabulary need not be condemned in themselves (e.g. in the work of great literary men like
Milton and Dr Johnson), it is of course possible to cover up emptiness of thought by using this vocabulary, and even (consciously
or unconsciously) to deny access to ideas to those who have not had
the necessary classical education. The purist tradition in English
letters (of which Orwell is partly an inheritor) has always opposed
wholesale use of classical vocabulary and has recommended
reliance on Anglo-Saxon words. In the nineteenth century some
scholars of language and literature went to great extremes in object-
ing to foreign borrowing in English. In so doing, they appear to
have been motivated, like Orwell, by objections to over-centralised
and 'artificial' forms of language, and they tended to view the real
and 'natural' form of language as being in the vernacular speech
of ordinary people. For a discussion of this tradition see J. Milroy
(1977).

Orwell may not have known the work of Whorf (d. 1941) or
Sapir (d. 1939) and may independently have come to the conclusion
that language can corrupt thought. Sapir and Whorf did not, of
course, speak of *corruption*. One of their points was that some
languages have grammatical structures that may condition their
speakers to think in ways that differ from European ways. The
language of the Hopi Indians, for instance (Whorf, 1941), has a
verbal system that is arranged in terms of types of movement
(spirals, curves and so on) rather than in terms of time distinctions

(past, present and future). It might be argued therefore that the language system of Hopi is more suitable than English for subjects like physics. Language scholars do not now accept the Sapir-Whorf hypothesis in its strong form: obviously, it can be pointed out that advances in physics have actually been made in Western European languages and not in Hopi, and that English (however its verb system is arranged) is just as capable of being used to express types of movement as any other language. We can afford to be rather less pessimistic than Orwell was about the possibility of an authoritarian government completely and permanently removing all possibility of creative thought from a language.

In 'Newspeak' Orwell considers the possibility that extreme authoritarian prescription could actually affect language quite radically at the level of *system* rather than merely at the level of *use*. He represents government intervention as fixing the meanings of words in purely literal senses. Thus, for example, the word *free* can be used in 'Newspeak' in a literal way in reference to a physical event, such as letting an animal go 'free' from a trap, but it cannot take on transferred, metaphorical and abstract meanings, for example to refer to 'freedom from tyranny'. Thus notions like political freedom and other ideas that might help people to think abstractly are effectively suppressed from the language and therefore from thought.

The authorities in *Nineteen Eighty-Four* had not merely interfered with words; they had interfered with abstract sense relations and processes that underlie the use of words and form the semantic structure of a language. They even seem to have suppressed systems of antonyms: the opposite of *good* was not *bad*, but the simple negative *ungood*. It is inconceivable that government intervention in *language use* could actually go as far as this: no language could be limited and fixed to the extent that transfer of meaning and figurative use of vocabulary could not take place. It is true that an authoritarian government can directly limit freedom of thought and public expression of ideas, but it cannot directly intervene in language structure in order to destroy the human capacity to exploit linguistic resources. All languages change and vary despite attempts to fix and standardise them. Orwell's 'Newspeak' exemplifies an impossible extreme of the prescriptive ideology.

Orwell's basic complaints were actually about society, morality and politics, and he chose language as a means of criticising society. He exhorts us to use the language carefully and precisely and to be critical about cliché and jargon in the use of language. In a much less spectacular way than that envisaged in *Nineteen Eighty-Four*, Orwell was of course right: we can be lulled into complacency through manipulative use of language by politicians and others on the mass media. One politician may be said to have *refuted* ('disproved') the argument of another when he has merely denied it; the murder of a village postman in Ulster may be reported as an *assassination*; destruction of Vietnamese villages may be described as *pacification*. Creeping paralysis in the understanding of events as reported through language, and ultimately in the use of certain parts of the language, can indeed be induced by centralised and public manipulation of language. The fault, however, does not lie in the language itself: it lies in the way that certain resources of language are being used and passively received. It is always possible for those resources to be used in responsible, thoughtful and critical ways.

Other complaints about careless and inaccurate use of a standard literary language do not usually have the depth, breadth and incisiveness of Orwell's complaints. Whereas others are often inclined to accept a certain degree of authoritarianism without necessarily reflecting on its implications, Orwell's ultimate position is anti-authoritarian and in favour of the ordinary user of language. In the next section, we shall see that similar concerns about effectiveness and clarity play some part in the views of educators in the teaching of literacy; however they can sometimes become confused with the concerns of Type 1 complaints on 'correctness'.

2.5 Standardisation and the teaching of literacy

It is probable that judgments about clarity and effectiveness in the use of language are universal to all human societies. In pre-literate societies, for example, it appears that it is not different *varieties* of language that are judged as 'better' or 'worse': judgments are confined to whether or not a given speaker communicates effectively and clearly (Mühlhäusler, 1982). To some extent, the kind of language criticism represented in Orwell's work is the same as this. Complaints about *correctness*, however, are typically found in communities that have highly developed standard languages, and we have suggested that the function of these complaints is to maintain public acceptance of one variety as superior to others. Unfortunately, these two separate concerns often become confused in public debates about the state of the language and the state of English teaching.

In recent years, there has been a great deal of public discussion about the teaching of English in schools. In the 1950s and 1960s, following the early work of Basil Bernstein, educationalists seized on language use as a way of explaining the failure of many working-class children to do well at school. They made use of Bernstein's distinction between the 'context-tied' restricted code and the 'context-free' elaborated code: working-class children, it was claimed, made relatively little use of the elaborated code, and it was sometimes believed that they did not have access to it. Thus, educational failure could be explained as due to unwillingness or inability to switch linguistically away from conversational language (in which mutual knowledge and background information are taken for granted) into something more like the language of prose (the context-free elaborated code). Clearly, Bernstein's distinction has much in common with a distinction that we shall make in Chapter 3 between informal conversational speech on the one hand and writing on the other. The difficulties that children face at school might indeed be better explained by a theory based on standardisation, such as we are developing in this book.

At about the same time, however, the teaching of traditional grammar declined in our school-system. This appears to have had serious consequences in language teaching generally, not because traditional grammar was abandoned, but because it was not immediately replaced by an equally good or better system of describing linguistic forms. Advances made by linguists in descriptive grammar have not for the most part been understood outside linguistics. Indeed, as we have seen in Chapter 1 general linguists are sometimes actually blamed for what has often been seen as a decline in standards of English teaching.

Problems in teaching the mother tongue have given rise to certain complaints, the main features of which have much in common with the complaint tradition. The first characteristic of this is a conviction that standards are declining and that they were at one time higher than they are now. In an article in the *Observer* (7 February 1982), John Rae, the Head Master of Westminster School, complains that there is a decline in literacy. A second characteristic of the tradition is that someone or something has to be blamed for the supposed decline. Rae blames the abandonment of formal grammar teaching and its replacement with creative writing teaching.

His article contains some other interesting arguments: for example, he claims that it is working-class children who have suffered the consequences of this decline: 'to working-class children the English language was an essential tool if they wanted to get on; if they were denied this and other basic skills they would effectively be kept in their place.' Another interesting feature of Rae's argument is the association of language and morality:

> The overthrow of grammar coincided with the acceptance of the equivalent of creative writing in social behaviour. As nice points of grammar were mockingly dismissed as pedantic and irrelevant, so was punctiliousness in such matters as honesty, responsibility, property, gratitude, apology and so on.

Compare the views of Swift (1712), who, in a longer analysis of the causes of linguistic corruption, had this to say: 'To this succeeded that Licentiousness which entered with the *Restoration*, and from infecting our Religion and Morals, fell to corrupt our Language' (Bolton, 1966: 112). There is little that is new in the complaint tradition.

As Rae's arguments appear at first sight to be very plausible it is important that we point out some difficulties. The first difficulty is in Rae's presupposition that there has been a general decline in literacy since about 1960. There is no very good reason to think that general standards of literacy have ever been very high: the bulk of our population over the past few generations has been able to read and write, but relatively few have achieved high levels of literacy. In recent years, tertiary education has greatly expanded: a higher proportion of the population is therefore likely to have attained a reasonably high standard of literacy. It is extremely difficult to estimate degrees and standards of literacy for whole populations, but the probability is that Rae is not correct.

The second difficulty concerns the reasoning of Rae's argument, and we shall discuss this in more detail. Repeatedly in his article, he associates 'grammar' (the substance of type 1 complaints) with effective writing (cf. Orwell and type 2 complaints). 'For nearly two decades', he states, '*formal grammar* and *the accurate use of language* have been anathema to most teachers of English in schools' (our italics). We would certainly agree that effective teaching of descriptive grammar should return to the curriculum, but if there is any relation between grammar teaching and skill in writing, it could well be an indirect one. The teaching of grammar *may* encourage a respect for precision and care, and it lays an essential basis for the teaching of foreign languages, but it has never been demonstrated that it is the main element in teaching effective writing skills. If, however, Rae does not mean 'grammar' at all but 'correct usage', that is another matter. Written English differs from spoken English, and there are perfectly grammatical spoken sequences that are simply not acceptable in writing (see Chapter 4). Handbooks such as that of Gowers (1954), as recommended by Rae, are excellent aids to good writing, but they are not books of 'grammar'.

The point is that Rae's argument is confused. Good writing will not necessarily follow on the heels of grammar teaching; furthermore, it is not clear whether Rae means 'grammar' or 'correct written usage'. If he means the latter, there are further implications, to which we now turn.

As we have seen, prescriptive notions of correctness tend in practice to be rather narrow and seemingly intolerant (in the next chapter, we shall see that prescriptions appropriate to the written channel are often uncritically applied to spoken usage). If, as Rae correctly argues, all children (including working-class children) should have equal access in principle to standard written English, it is important that the differences between speech and writing should be clearly pointed out and that spoken forms should not be devalued (cf. the views of Orwell).

Yet, underlying these apparently simple recommendations, there is a huge problem that is of a social or sociolinguistic kind rather than narrowly linguistic. Language use is embedded in a social matrix, and, as we suggested in 1.2, privately held attitudes to language are not necessarily identical with those publicly expressed by the guardians or the complaint tradition. Sociolinguists have shown that many close-knit communities place a higher value on oral skills than on written ones (Labov, 1972b; L. Milroy, 1980); we shall discuss in Chapter 3 the community pressures that tend to maintain these values and also maintain the forms of non-standard English (symbolising community identities). Children who want 'to get on' (as Rae puts it) may face a considerable dilemma, as 'getting on' may involve distancing from family and friends, or, as we have elsewhere described it (L. Milroy, 1980: 194–8), opting for *status* and rejecting *solidarity*. We shall not get far in English teaching if these problems and their effects on language use are not initially recognised. Failure to address them will merely maintain the *status quo*.

2.6   Conclusions

In this section we shall briefly summarise the main points that arise from this chapter.

We have continued to argue that standardisation is a process that is always present in the development of a major language, and that it is promoted through various channels. The standard ideology encourages prescription in language, dedicated to the principle that there must be one, and only one, correct way of using a linguistic item (at the level of pronunciation, spelling, grammar and, to a great extent, meaning). Attempts to prescribe standard usage in spoken language are never wholly successful, and quite unsuccessful at the level of pronunciation and grammar: however, the prescriptive tradition has succeeded in bringing about broad consensus on the norms of written language.

The first type of complaint tradition is dedicated to keeping the standard ideology alive, and is based on the assumption that the resources of standard English are inherently superior to those of other dialects. This is not necessarily the case. The reason for promoting one unitary dialect above the others is the desirability of uniformity. If usage is uniform, communication is more efficient and miscomprehension less likely. However, as we have noted, this tradition has not been noticeably successful in reducing variability in speech (as against writing).

The second type of complaint is not primarily concerned with non-standard usage, but with observed abuses in public and formal language, usually written, and always standardised in its basic structure. This type of criticism assumes that a standard literary language already exists and the function of the tradition is to promote clarity of usage and careful thinking about choice of words. Its recommendations are clearly relevant to an education in literacy. As we shall see in Chapter 3, fluency in written language requires different types of skills from fluency in speech, and careful training is needed. It is important also that a population should be capable of being critical and perceptive about public use of language on the part of politicians and others: Orwell was clearly concerned about this. We would suggest that the linguistic criticism of this tradition is infinitely more important for our educational system than are the more arid and pedantic aspects of grammatical 'correctness' as promoted by the first type of complaint. So too are the well informed and carefully reasoned arguments of linguists such as Stubbs (1983b) and Sinclair (1982).

Public discussion of the 'Standard English' issue in schools has been less reflective and less well informed about language than it ought to be. The distinctions between language system and language use, and between speech and writing, have seldom been adequately emphasised, and there has been confusion between 'grammatical correctness' and 'effective writing'. The arguments of language scholars such as Stubbs and Sinclair are not usually acknowledged in these public discussions: they are not publicised in the press, as the views of Rae (1982) and Honey (1983) are. The educational importance of these matters, however, is such that a higher level of public debate is essential. This is further discussed in Chapter 5 and elsewhere in this book.

3
Spoken and written norms

3.1 Introduction

In Chapters 1 and 2 we have been largely concerned with attitudes to language, especially with the effects of the standard ideology on public expressed attitudes. We have noted that the most fully described and codified forms of language are those appropriate to public, formal and, especially, written usage. One effect of this has been a neglect of the structure and social dynamics of spoken forms and hence a tendency (in the absence of adequate descriptions of speech) to evaluate spoken usage on the model of written usage. In this chapter we focus on the relation between speech and writing, and differences in the forms and functions of the two channels of language.

It is appropriate to draw attention once more to the fact that there is much greater variability in speech than there is in written language. This variability can be traced, or described, in at least three dimensions: geographical, social and situational. Spoken language varies regionally, it varies according to social grouping of speakers, and it varies in the speech of individuals according to the situational contexts in which they find themselves from time to time. Some consequences of this variability are examined in this chapter and are further discussed in subsequent chapters.

Variation in the synchronic dimension is the counterpart of change in the diachronic dimension. Linguistic change, especially in phonology and grammar, originates in speech rather than in writing: it is thus characteristic of spoken forms to be perpetually in a state of change. The eighteenth-century prescribers and codifiers were well aware of this. Swift saw no reason *why* language should be allowed to change continuously, and Johnson spoke of 'fugitive cant' which was always 'in a state of increase or decay'

(Bolton, 1966: 150); he therefore preferred to codify the established literary part of the vocabulary, which he regarded as more 'durable'. In this chapter, we shall approach variability in speech by first considering the social factors that affect linguistic change in the spoken channel, and balancing these against the factors that encourage stability and resist change. The discussion then moves on to the relation between the written and spoken channels. We consider some consequences of evaluating speech according to written models and examine some differences in the forms and functions of speech and writing. The implications of these evaluations in education and language testing are more fully investigated in later chapters.

3.2 Language change and language maintenance

No one can fully explain why spoken language is perpetually changing (see discussions by Aitchison, 1981; Lass, 1980). Some approaches emphasise internal characteristics of the language system itself and do not look to social factors for the primary causes of change. Languages, however, do not exist independently of speakers, and if changes take place in them, such changes must be the reflexes of speaker-innovations, established as new norms by speaker acceptance. In other words, it does not seem possible to account fully for linguistic change (as observed in language systems) without inquiring into the social origins and social mechanisms of change. It is speakers who innovate in the first place — not languages.

In recent years it has been repeatedly demonstrated that observed linguistic changes often correlate with social factors. The spread of post-vocalic [r] in New York City, for example, has been shown to be connected with what Labov (1972a) has called hypercorrection by the lower middle class. Social correlations of change have also been investigated by Trudgill (1974), Milroy and Milroy (1978) and others. In a much wider time-scale than that considered in these recent studies, it is obvious that an explanation for the functional elaboration that took place in the history of English vocabulary could not even be approached if we took no account of social and cultural changes in the history of England (Leith, 1983; J. Milroy, 1984)

Recent sociolinguistic research has focused on change in progress at the present day, and it has been largely concerned with pronunciation changes. Some changes such as the change in progress towards restoration of post-vocalic [r] (in *car*, *card*, etc.) in New York City (Labov, 1966, 1972a), seem to be motivated by status or prestige factors; other changes, however, do *not* seem to move in the direction of high-prestige or national standard pronunciations. Trudgill (1974) demonstrates that centralisation of $/\varepsilon/$ before $/l/$ in such words as *help* (in which *help* sounds a little like *hulp*) is spreading in Norwich, even though it is hardly a 'standard' feature. Research in Belfast (Milroy and Milroy, 1978; L. Milroy, 1980; J. Milroy, 1981, 1982) has shown that at lower levels of society the pronunciation of $/a/$ (as in *bad*, *have*, *hat*, etc.) is moving away from 'front' values (as in RP *hat*), which we would normally associate with high prestige, towards 'back' values (as in RP *calm*); i.e. speakers prefer to pronounce *bad*, *have*, etc. with a vowel similar to that in RP *calm*. A simple prestige model (from high to low status) does not seem to be sufficient to give a sociolinguistic explanation for change: it appears that we must also consider how norms *other than* those of the 'standard' can be maintained over periods of time and how (paradoxically) differential maintenance at different times and places can itself give rise to observed contrast and variation between different regional and social dialects.

Linguistic change is not unconstrained, and adequate accounts of change must, amongst other things, consider the social factors that resist change and maintain norms. We shall call this latter tendency *maintenance*, and begin by postulating that *maintenance* is the converse of change. There are social mechanisms that encourage change (e.g. the overt or covert prestige attached to certain pronunciations), and other social mechanisms that seek to stabilise a language or dialect, and in so doing impede or prevent linguistic change.

It is convenient to distinguish two kinds of mechanism that tend to encourage stability in the use of a language or dialect. Both may apply at any level of society, but one or other may be dominant at some levels. The first mechanism is *covert* and *informal* pressure for language maintenance, which is exerted by members of one's peer-group or social group. The second is *overt* and *institutional* enforcement of norms through public channels such as the educational and broadcasting systems. We shall first consider *covert* and informal mechanisms.

Previously, we attempted to account for covert maintenance

by appealing to the notion of social network (L. Milroy, 1980); an approach based on social network attempted to answer the question: why do people continue to use low status varieties when they know that it may well be in their economic and social interests to acquire a variety of high prestige? It seems to be true that low prestige varieties (although changing in the course of time) can persist as distinct from the standard over long periods of time. Social network theory proposes that varieties of language are subject to maintenance through pressure exerted by informal ties of kin and friendship.

These informal pressures are likely to be strong when the personal ties involved are *dense* and *multiplex*. A network can be described as *dense* when, in a given group of persons, virtually everybody knows everybody else. Ties of this kind typically exist in small territorial communities such as villages and in well-defined urban communities ('urban villages' and ghettoes). But they may also exist at higher levels of society, e.g. in professional sub-groups and in upper-class society, where contacts may be maintained over long distances owing to important common interests.

The degree of network *multiplexity*, however, is probably highest when the group concerned is territorially based (i.e. in low status groups). *Multiplexity* attempts to measure the *strength* of the ties (as distinct from the number of ties) that exist between individuals within the network. Whereas *density* is based on whether or not A knows B, C, D and E and whether they all know one another, a *multiplexity* measure estimates the *number* of capacities in which A knows B, or C, or D. Thus, A may know B as a relative, friend, neighbour and workmate, and also C, D, E in a similar number of capacities.

Density and multiplexity of networks constrain the behaviour of individuals within the networks. For example, if the network is dense and multiplex, A will have to be careful about spreading a rumour about B, as he knows that the information will rapidly become common knowledge in the network. If he does wish to spread the rumour, he will have to calculate whether it will be believed, and whether the consequences of his action will be beneficial or damaging to him. Another kind of behaviour that is constrained by the network is the use of colloquial pronunciation, grammar and vocabulary.

If a member of a close-knit working-class group begins to adopt speech that is not exactly the common speech of the network (e.g.

if he says *I saw* rather than *I seen* or begins to use initial [h] when his peers do not use it), he must again weigh up the potential benefits and disadvantages of this behaviour. To the extent that he values the moral, emotional and practical support of his network peers, he will opt for their familiar speech-patterns. To the extent that he chooses the standardised or high-prestige form of the language, he is opting for *status* rather than solidarity. In so doing, he is taking a decision to distance himself from the norms of his group in the interests of his own social mobility. Our research in inner-city Belfast suggested that it was quite rare in these working-class groups for a person to prefer status to solidarity. Even those who had the potential to benefit economically from participation in the educational system did not usually wish to leave the security of their home communities: this was reflected in their speech in addition to other aspects of their behaviour. Social network theory, therefore, seems to have provided some insight into why low-status local and regional varieties have such a strong capacity to persist despite the institutional pressures that favour Standard English. It is obviously important that the implications of this should be understood by educators and others.

If the variety concerned happens to be regarded as the standard language, there may again be informal pressures (in addition to institutional pressures) that tend to maintain it. For example, English RP was maintained between the late nineteenth century until well after the Second World War as an élite and exclusive accent partly through ties formed by members of the élite group at school, university, clubs, in the army and so on. An approach based on network analysis would propose that this common language was maintained because of the common interests of these groups. But a standard language is additionally maintained in an official and institutional way. It is the official language, used by government; it is codified in dictionaries and grammar-books; it is appealed to as the norm in the educational system. These facts give it a *legitimacy* that other varieties do not usually have and make it *potentially* accessible to all citizens. While non-standard norms are maintained to some extent by disapproval of deviations from those norms (consider, for example, the Belfast youth who reported that he was physically assaulted for pronouncing the word *pull* in the standard rather than the non-standard way: L. Milroy, 1980; J. Milroy, 1981), standard norms are additionally maintained by institutional authority. As we saw in Chapter 2, even those who write to the papers complaining about some supposed misuse of language are attempting to contribute to the maintenance of the standard by appealing to authority and effectively keeping the norms of the high-status variety alive.

These various different pressures on language use obviously have not resulted in the total uniformity that is required by the ideology of standardisation. The great regional and social diversity that exists in spoken English usage arises partly from the fact that language is always in a state of change and that regional dialects tend to diverge from one another. Paradoxically, it also seems to arise partly from the desire to maintain norms. To the extent that localised pressures for maintenance differ in their aims from those of the standard ideology, there is a permanent tension between language use that is maintained by solidarity pressures and usage that is maintained, or enforced, by status-based ideologies. Despite the great improvements in communication that have come about in the last two centuries, these competing pressures seem to have had the effect of maintaining greater diversity in spoken English usage than the standard ideology would require (see further the discussion of 'social norms' and 'community norms' in Chapter 6).

3.3 Spoken English and the effects of literacy

In the previous section, we were concerned with the effects of change and maintenance on *spoken* language rather than written language. In that section, and in previous chapters, we have generally referred to written language in terms of its importance in the ideology of standardisation. One function of written language and the writing system (its conventions of spelling, grammar and word-choice) is to enforce or maintain standardisation. Furthermore, as we have seen, it is only in the writing system that a high degree of uniformity has been achieved. The ideology of standardisation has been less successfully applied to spoken language, which continues to be subject to quite extensive variation and change.

One reason why the norms of colloquial English grammar have not been so successfully standardised is that they have not in the past been so fully *described* as the norms of written English have been: for this reason it has not been possible to codify them to the same extent. The very considerable differences that exist between modes of sentence construction in speech and writing have been touched upon sporadically, but handbooks of usage have been based much more on the norms of writing, and have taken relatively formal registers of English as their main reference point. Even in linguistic theory (see below), the underlying models and the data used for grammatical argumentation have been largely based on relatively formal and 'careful' usage. This is only to be expected, as it has been difficult until quite recently to study speech in any depth. In the last few decades, however, the availability of tape-recorders has made it possible to collect extensive samples of spoken language and to analyse them in much greater detail than was previously possible.

Although great advances have been made since about 1960 in the study of spoken language, language scholars still rely to some extent on an inheritance handed down from the past. Chomsky's transformational-generative grammar, for instance, which had its first impact in the early 1960s, elevated the armchair linguist to a position of pre-eminence in the subject and was actively hostile to a corpus-based linguistics (the approach which uses a body of real data). Before that time, little scholarly attention had been given to the *spoken* forms of major European languages: the fieldwork that had been done had either been mainly devoted to collecting single words in isolation (as in regional dialectology), or to investigating 'exotic' pre-literary languages such as American Indian languages (see e.g. Whorf, 1956). Under Chomsky's influence, the transformational linguists of the 1960s believed that the native speaker's intuitions about grammaticality in English were reliable, so they exemplified their arguments by using idealised sentences made up out of their heads: many of the sentences they judged to be ungrammatical were, in fact, possible and grammatical in some variety of English other than their own. Naturally, the sentence types that were considered to be grammatical were normally standard English types. Furthermore, they often had a literary or formal air and seemed unlikely to occur often in everyday speech.

Transformational generative grammar is not the only approach to language that has until recently been strongly influenced by the consequences of literacy. Historical linguistics, for instance, even though it has always insisted on the primacy of speech, has often lost its way and produced historical accounts of English and other languages that are largely focused on the development of the standard literary language.

Even H.C. Wyld (1927:16), who elsewhere insisted that the

historical language studies must focus on the *speech* of the past
(rather than writing), had this to say:

> Fortunately, at the present time, the great majority of English
> Dialects are of very little importance as representatives of
> English speech, and...we can afford to let them go, except in so
> far as they throw light upon the growth of those forms of our
> language which are the main objects of our solicitude, namely,
> the language of Literature and Received Standard Spoken
> English.

It is only in recent years that we have realised how great are the
differences between spoken and written languages, and this advance in our knowledge has been made possible by the availability
of the tape-recorder. The analysis of real speech in conversational
contexts can throw light on both present and past states of language
(Labov, 1974; J. Milroy, 1984c).

If linguists have been quite slow to understand the importance of
speech/writing differences and their practical implications, the
general public (including other professionals) has been much
slower. We live in a society that places considerable emphasis on
literacy, and much of our schooling is devoted to the acquisition of
literacy. As a result, many of the handbook prescriptions on 'correct' English (which influence our attitudes to usage) are concerned
primarily with correct *written* English, and not directly with
speech. From many thousands of major and minor instances, we
shall consider two.

Fowler (1926) has an interesting entry on sentences of the type:
He only died yesterday, which occur frequently in *speech* of standard and non-standard speakers. The objection to the sentence is
that the adverb, *only*, is placed in a position where the sentence
could mean 'All that he did yesterday was die' when it 'really'
means 'It was only yesterday that he died': the word-order results
in a potential ambiguity. This potential ambiguity is of little or no
importance in speech, as the social context and mutual knowledge
of speakers, together with stress and intonation, will make the
intended meaning clear. There will be no breakdown of efficient
communication (for a discussion see also Bolinger, 1980:6).
Writing, however, is deprived of stress, intonation and the
possibility of immediate feedback from speakers: to write a
language well is a continuous struggle against ambiguity. In written

prose, therefore, a potential ambiguity of the kind discussed is functionally inefficient: the sentence may be wrongly understood.

Our first example applies to standard as well as non-standard speech: our second example is based on what has become non-standard in recent centuries: the double or multiple negative (e.g. *I never said nothing*). Until the early seventeenth century, multiple negation was normal in literary English, and it remains normal in the standard forms of many other languages, e.g. Spanish: *no es nada*, lit. 'it isn't nothing'. Its later exclusion from written English seems to have something to do with the development of English prose-writing (based as it partly was on the clause and phrase structures of Latin literary prose, in which multiple negation was prohibited). However, it is again clear that potential ambiguity in writing could be responsible for this prohibition as a sentence like *He didn't say nothing* could well be open to either a positive (i.e. 'he said something') or a negative (i.e. 'he said nothing') interpretation in a piece of writing that is, by definition, deprived of stress, intonation, and other cues that can assist comprehension.

It is possible that a majority of all English speakers use multiple negation in speech, despite the efforts of prescribers and correctors. This is not to say that these speakers use multiple negation all the time: they probably switch between simple and multiple negation. A socially neutral approach to this requires us to consider the possibility that multiple negation is an additional resource of speech and not a defect due to ignorance or illogicality. *It ain't no cat can't get in no coop* (quoted by Labov, 1972b:130, from a speaker of Black English) may not be considered elegant in writing; but in the circumstances the speaker expressed his point more emphatically than if he had said *There isn't any cat that can get into any coop*: he leaves us in no doubt that the pigeon-coop is extremely safe. The removal of multiple negation from the grammar of writing may have been justified in some ways, but its removal from speech may also have meant the loss of a device that could be used for emphasis.

These two examples have been used in an attempt to demonstrate that many prescriptive 'rules' are in the first place devised as guidelines for composing clear and unambiguous written English: if they are applied critically, they are important in the teaching and acquisition of literacy. However, the guardians of the language have often lost sight of the fact that such 'rules' are only guidelines (sometimes outdated ones) for efficient communication in writing and in the most careful kind of public speaking. Narrow and uncritical application of such rules may reduce potential for effective communication, especially in conversation and at less formal levels of usage. We shall return to this point in Chapter 4.

Section 3.4 is devoted to a more detailed review of the formal and functional differences between the spoken and written channels; in this the influence of prescriptive norms remains a major theme.

3.4 The spoken and written channels

Although spoken language is diverse in its forms and functions, the norms of written grammar, spelling and vocabulary are much more uniform. As we have seen, the appeal to the authority of written usage is one way in which standardisation of speech is promoted. But we have also emphasised that the forms and functions of spoken language are very largely different from those of writing. These differences are now considered in greater detail.

The most obvious differences between speech and writing are *formal*. Speech is an auditory medium: it is produced orally and received by the ear; writing is a visual medium; it is produced manually and received by the eye. While speech activity can rely on a number of situational factors to help to convey meaning and intention, the act of writing is deprived of an immediate context of communication. It is most important that we recognise the implications of this difference. When we speak, we constantly use *paralinguistic* features to help us: these can be vocal (tone of voice, intonation, pause, emphasis) or non-vocal (gesture, facial expression). We may also rely on unspoken knowledge in order to interpret what is being said: if we overhear a conversation, it may well be difficult to understand what it is about unless we share in the mutual prior knowledge of the participants. Speaking, then, is a *social* activity, whereas writing is *solitary*. It follows, therefore, that whereas vagueness, ellipsis and ambiguity can be tolerated in speech to a high degree (because mistakes and miscomprehensions can often be repaired if they should occur at all), they can sometimes be quite properly criticised when they appear in writing. It may be adequate for a speaker to refer to someting in the situational context as *that over there* or to some person merely as *him* or *her*; but this will obviously not do for a writer, for the reason that writing is deprived of a situational context and gives no opportunity for exchange of comments between participants. Objects, persons, concepts, events and actions must all be carefully specified in writing. The general view that writing is a more 'careful' activity than speech is broadly true, except in so far as some non-conversational speech ('spoken prose', e.g. lectures, sermons) is similar to writing in this respect (see Chapter 7). Writing is normally *planned* (cf. lectures, etc.) whereas conversation is *unplanned*. Note also that the distinction we are suggesting between writing as relatively *context-free* and speech as relatively *context-tied* is the same as one of those made by Bernstein (1971, etc.) between 'elaborated' and 'restricted' codes (see Chapter 7).

We have already indicated that speech and writing have different *functions*. Conversational speech is social, and everyday conversation is an exchange between participants: speech is used to pass the time of day ('It's a pleasant evening isn't it?'), to request actions ('Put your coat on the hanger'), to acquire information ('Can you give me the time, please?'), to convey emotions and attitudes ('You have the most beautiful eyes I've ever seen') and for an enormous variety of other purposes. But speech is ephemeral – it dies away as soon as it is uttered – and the basic function of writing is to overcome to some extent the impermanence of speech. Written language has traditionally been used to keep records of all kinds, and written documents have facilitated communication over long distances and long periods of time. Our access to history is mainly through writing.

Writing, however, is not a 'natural' activity in quite the same way that speech is. Speech is acquired by all normally endowed human beings without explicit instruction, whereas writing has to be taught *after* the basic grammar, phonology and lexicon of spoken language have already been largely mastered. In the experience of the child, writing is built up on already acquired knowledge of speech. Whereas writing can be described as an art or a skill that is not universal to all human societies, speech is not fundamentally an art, but an innate human capacity that *is* universal to all societies. As writing skills are difficult, our educational systems have concentrated on inculcating a relatively high degree of literacy, with little attention paid to the nature of spoken language as an everyday social activity. Training in the use of 'English' (in 'O' level examinations, for instance) is usually assumed to be training in the use of *written* English and training in the acquisition of the elaborated vocabulary of standard English. At a higher level, the study of 'English' in the sixth form and universities is largely the study of English literature and literary criticism. Spoken language is taken for granted. As a result of this constant emphasis on written language, there is an understandable tendency for people to believe that writing is somehow more complicated and difficult (and more important) than speech. The *functional* importance of literacy in the development of western civilisation has been so great that very high values are placed on the written channel, and it is usually considered (implicitly or explicitly) to be 'superior' to speech. Indeed, when language critics write about the decline of 'English' (as they often do), they almost always assume (without explanation) that the 'language' referred to is written or formal English of some kind. Ian Robinson's book *The Survival of English* (1973), for example, does not literally contemplate the possible demise of the language as a whole (as Dorian's *Language Death* (1981) does for Scots Gaelic), but is concerned with public and formal usage only.

This emphasis on literacy (and corresponding neglect of the study of speech) has affected our beliefs about *spoken* English and, in some particulars, has actually affected our use of spoken English (as in 'spelling-pronunciation', e.g. restoring the [h] in words such as *herb, humour, humble, hotel*, which were [h]-less in the original French and remained so in English for many centuries. Even though speech and writing are different in form and function, the norms of written prose are often held up as models for 'correct' speech in a variety of ways.

The reasons for this have already been considered in a general way: it is now appropriate to review them in the light of what has been discussed in this chapter. First, we may note that it has not been possible until recently to carry out research into conversational speech in any detail; as a result traditional handbooks of usage have been largely based on the norms of writing, which have been more fully described. Second the written medium is characteristically standardised, i.e. it is intolerant of optional variability in the structural characteristics of language: consequently this intolerance has been carried over into prescriptive pronouncements on usage, and has been to some extent applied to speech. It is now appropriate to emphasise the great uniformity of written language in certain aspects.

Standardisation of the written language is easiest to demonstrate with reference to orthography: spelling is the most uniform level of language use, and contrasts in this respect with the variability of its counterpart in speech − pronunciation. However, the principle of uniformity in usage applies also to other levels of linguistic organisation, e.g. sentence-construction. We now briefly consider the English spelling system and pass on from this to consider the principle of invariance in prescriptive views of sentence structure.

Twentieth century English spelling is almost absolutely invariant. In earlier times, a limited number of alternants were acceptable, and informal spelling (e.g. in personal letters) remained relatively free even in the eighteenth century. The idea of an absolutely fixed spelling system is recent; particular spellings of words are now regarded as *uniquely* acceptable, other possible spellings being rejected as 'errors'. Yet, although particular 'correct' spellings can often be shown to be motivated by historical factors, so also can some 'incorrect' alternants. The accepted orthography is ultimately arbitrary and fixed by convention. It is not permissible to spell ordinary words like *soap*, *eat*, *owl* as 'sope', 'eet', 'oul', even though rhyming words may employ these latter conventions, e.g. *hope*, *feet*, *foul* (indeed Dr. Johnson accepted *soap/sope* and *choak/choke* as alternants). It cannot be said that the accepted spellings are in themselves more logical than the unacceptable ones, as both sets bear the same relation to the phonology: *soap* rhymes with *hope*, *eat* with *feet*, and so on. Over the centuries, uniquely correct spellings have been promoted largely through the activities of publishing houses, and equally 'logical' alternants have been rejected. The idea that a linguistic form can be uniquely correct and other 'equally good' forms incorrect is thus seen at its clearest in spelling (on the history of spelling, see Scragg, 1975).

The same principle however also applies to written syntax and morphology. Uniquely correct forms have been prescribed in prose-writing since the eighteenth century, and other equivalent forms prohibited. The choice of *different from* in preference to *different to* or *different than*, for example, is (as we have seen) ultimately arbitrary, although various attempts have been made to rationalise the choice.

Notice that prescriptive preference for one form over another depends on the assumption that the alternants are exactly equivalent, as in *different from* as against *different to*. That is probably why it has been possible to standardise spelling so successfully: there can be no doubt that two spellings such as *soap/sope* are exactly equivalent: they refer to the same lexical item. In sentence-construction and word-construction, however, one cannot usually be so certain that two expressions are exactly equivalent, and in the next chapter we examine certain cases where prescriptive writers have lost sight of this principle of equivalence. The present discussion is confined to cases in which alternative constructions *are* equivalent: our point is that the *invariance* that is in principle necessary in the written medium is, in prescriptive writing, often taken as a model for speech.

The right way to improve your English, by J.E. Metcalfe, first appeared as an inexpensive paperback in 1963 and has been reprinted several times. Metcalfe's pronouncements typically make no distinction between writing and speech, and the prescriptions are absolute. Thus (Metcalfe, 1975:150) states that 'In spite of various feeble attempts at defence, "different to" is wrong simply because it is illogical. Nobody would dream of *saying* "similar from"'. (Our italics). Similarly, the following refers indifferently to speech and writing: 'You are not *averse to* or show an *aversion to* anything. The suffix [*sic*] *to* signifies approach, when the opposite is intended. You can only be *averse from* or show an *aversion from*, something.'

Notice that, although these pronouncements make the familiar appeals to logic and etymology, they embody an assumption that certain variants must be suppressed. Whether the author is conscious of it or not, they are directed at standardisation, which, as we have seen, is most accessible in the written channel.

In quoting these examples, we are not concerned with arbitrating between two usages. We have merely attempted to demonstrate that, just as dictionaries prescribe uniquely correct spellings, so handbooks of usage prescribe uniquely correct grammatical constructions, when there may be a choice of two or more equally serviceable constructions in current spoken use. The best handbooks, however, often recognise that their function is to help the *writer* rather than the speaker (see, for example, Gowers, 1954), or make careful attempts to distinguish between written and spoken usage and between various levels of formality in usage (e.g. Fowler, 1926). But the doctrine of linguistic absoluteness dies hard, and these relevant distinctions are frequently *not* made. Examples of insensitivity to levels of usage are easy to find.

One obvious fact of spoken usage is that speakers have the capacity to make alternative choices according to situational context, and that they may exploit these choices in order to achieve varying effects (see Chapter 6 on 'communicative competence'). In

British English, for example, an inquiry about speaker-identity on the telephone normally takes the form: *Who am I speaking to?*; the so-called preposition is at the end of the utterance. However, if the situation is perceived as formal, *or if frigidity and social distance is deliberately intended*, the form: *To whom am I speaking?* may be preferred. Such subtleties of speaker-variation mean nothing to the narrower forms of the prescriptive tradition. Consider Metcalfe again (1975:132): '"Who shall I give it to?" is wrong because the question is another form of "I shall give it to whom?" or "To whom shall I give it?" ... a preposition ... is followed by the objective.' The prescription is, once again, absolute, and no allowance is made for situational variation in speech.

3.5   Conclusions

The argument of this chapter has focused on the nature of speech as against writing. Whereas the writing system requires a high degree of uniformity so that messages may be transmitted over time and distance in a clear and unambiguous manner, speech is a social activity. The seeds of change are always present in spoken languages, and even the social factors that encourage covert and informal maintenance of particular spoken varieties may have the effect of ensuring that different varieties continue to maintain partly independent existences. The standard ideology, however, promotes uniformity at the expense of variety, and the prescriptive tradition has always aimed at uniformity in speech as well as writing.

Attempts to prescribe uniformity in speech have not, however, been noticeably successful, and this arises (at least partly) from the failure of the tradition to take account of the fact that variability in speech is partly a result of social factors. It also arises, partly, from the functions of speech. That is to say that the existence of alternative choices (e.g. in sentence construction) contributes to the communicative competence of speakers: they may exploit these choices for different social purposes, and the existence of alternatives is in such cases functional. The narrower forms of prescription may therefore be seen as 'diseases' or malfunctions of the ideology of standardisation, arising from ignorance of the nature of speech, which leads to uncritical applications of the principle of uniformity to inappropriate cases.

In the next chapter, we continue to examine the forms of speech in the light of the prescriptive tradition. We shall consider selected aspects of the grammar of colloquial English, beginning with examples that are normally considered 'standard' (in a loose sense): we than extend the discussion to the grammar of non-standard English. In later chapters, we go on to consider the variability of speech in other dimensions – e.g. in the ability of speakers to vary their speech according to different situational contexts, and at all times we bear in mind the consequences of the narrow application of the standard ideology.

4
Grammar and speech

4.1 Introduction

This chapter is about the grammar of speech, and it continues naturally from the topic of Chapter 3, in which the formal and functional differences between speech and writing were discussed. Having noted that one of the less fortunate consequences of standardisation is the application of the norms of writing to the grammar of speech, we begin by discussing the nature of 'grammar' and pass on to consider some *misapplications* of prescriptive norms to spoken English. In Section 4.3 the dimension of contextual variability in speech is considered, again bearing in mind the effect on speech of the relatively inflexible norms of prescriptive written grammar. As non-standard English is (almost by definition) spoken rather than written, the discussion is then extended to the grammaticality of non-standard English. Throughout this chapter, it should be borne in mind that no full and authoritative description of spoken English grammar is available. The examples used are therefore selective, but they are based very largely on real data systematically collected.

Grammar, in the popular view (and this is based on the standard ideology), is believed to consist of a number of 'rules' that are imposed on usage from outside, for example by some authority on correctness. These rules are largely a set of prohibitions against particular expressions (such as *different to*) that are recurrent and persistent. The grammar of a language or dialect is actually something much more wide-ranging than this. It is a complex and abstract system inherent in the language and not imposed by overt prescription. All native speakers have implicit knowledge of the grammar of English: it is this knowledge that enables speakers to use and understand their language. Amongst other things, this knowledge enables the speaker to judge what sentences are possible in the language. For instance, native speakers intuitively know that Set 1 (below) consists of grammatical sequences and that Set 2 consists of ungrammatical sequences:

Set 1	Set 2
The white house	*The house white
John was hit by Jack	*Was hit by Jack John
Charlie died	*Died Charlie

These Set 1 sequences are grammatical, not because the order or choice of words is necessarily the best or the most 'logical', but because the rules of English grammar require these sequences. In other languages, the conventions may be different. French, for example, requires *the house white* ('la maison blanche'), and Gaelic requires *died Charlie* ('bhàsaich Tearlach').

The most general grammatical rules of a language, or dialect of a language, are learnt by the native speaker in infancy and childhood without explicit instruction; they are rules of speech. It is a fallacy to believe that most of language is learnt at school: children are taught *reading* and *writing* at school. The basic grammar of the spoken language has already been acquired by the time they go to school, i.e. children 'know' the main conventions and can put spoken sentences together according to 'correct' syntactic rules, even if their performance is imperfect in some details (e.g. the use of 'goed' for *went* or 'buyed' for *bought*). What they implicitly know about grammar at the age of five is infinitely greater than what they do not know. We now turn to some aspects of spoken usage and consider the relevance of prescriptive norms to those usages.

The differences between spoken and written grammar arise largely from the different properties and functions of the two channels. As speech is adapted to social use, certain kinds of sentence-structure are more common in speech than in writing, for example utterances that *point* to something in the environment and which therefore have a structure that we can broadly call 'topicalised': 'That's me in the photograph': 'This is the boy who stole the apples'. Another type of sentence that is more common in speech than in writing is the *elliptical* sentence. In reply to a question *Where is the squirrel?*, a speaker might answer: *In the tree*, deleting the noun-phrase and verb: *The squirrel is*.... He can do this because the topic has already been specified. Traditionally,

however, utterances like *In the tree* have been labelled incomplete
sentences and have even been said to be 'wrong'. The reason for
this, of course, is the traditional emphasis on writing and neglect
of speech; as writing is not so much assisted by immediate situational context, it is necessary to be more specific in writing than in
speech.

On the other hand, there are sentence-types that are more common in writing than in speech. Long complex sentences with
multiple embeddings of clauses are difficult for speakers to construct and to understand because of the limitations of human
memory; but they can be understood by readers, because readers
(unlike speakers) have time to interpret them.

4.2 Prescription and spoken language

Prescriptive rules have usually been devised in the first place for
writing rather than speech. If such rules are imposed on speech,
they may sometimes actually damage its expressive potential and
flexibility. This is particularly the case when the prescriptive pronouncements are mistaken or misleading, i.e. when the inflexibility
characteristic of such pronouncements goes too far.

The function of prescription is to normalise usage (especially in
writing): thus, as we have already noted; a prescriptive pronounce-
ment seeks to legitimise one out of two or more usages that are
equivalent in meaning (e.g. *different from* as against *different to* or
different than). The danger here is that the usages concerned may
not always be equivalent in meaning; hence, the prescriptive prohibition, if successful, may remove a resource from the language
that is possibly useful for distinguishing fine shades of meaning.
Thus the objection here is not to prescription in itself, but to the
narrow and uncritical application of prescriptive rules to spoken
usage. We now consider some examples.

Metcalfe (1975:145–6) objects to expressions like *face up to*,
stand for (approx. 'tolerate'), *slow down*, *try out*, which he
describes as 'hateful', 'horrible' and 'disreputable'. This type of
construction is, of course, particularly common in speech. Metcalfe
believes that these are unnecessary and that the simplex verb forms
face, *stand*, etc. have the same meanings. Thus, he claims, *I'm not
standing for* (i.e. 'tolerating') *it* has the same meaning as *I'm not
standing it*. The English language is much given to these verb-

particle combinations, and it is unlikely that there would be so many of them if they were not in some way functional and if their meanings were precisely the same as the simplex verbs. Indeed, it will be apparent from the sentences below that the distribution of *stand for* ('tolerate') is not quite the same as that of *stand* ('tolerate'). The 'doubtful' construction is asterisked:

1 (a) Bill can't stand Edward.
  (b) *Bill can't stand for Edward.

Furthermore, the meanings are different in the following:

2 (a) I won't stand another game of Monopoly.
  (b) I won't stand for another game of Monopoly.
3 (a) George stood Polly's impudence all morning.
  (b) George stood for Polly's impudence all morning.

In 2(a), there is a suggestion that the speaker will hardly survive another game of Monopoly, whereas in 2(b) there is a suggestion that he is positively forbidding it. The meaning of *stand* ('tolerate') in 2(a) and 3(a) appears to be close to 'suffer passively', whereas that of *stand for* (2b, 3b) is more positive: when we 'stand for' something we take a positive decision to put up with it. Therefore, the choice between *stand* and *stand for* is useful as it enables speakers to convey a subtle distinction of meaning. The prescriptive prohibition, in this case and in many others, is simply inappropriate, and the example discussed can be considered as a malfunction of the standard ideology.

4.3 Prescription and contextual variability in speech

Apart from appearing to inhibit flexibility in conveying meaning, prescriptive ideas of correctness can also interfere with a speaker's sense of appropriateness of language in varying situational contexts. There is no speaker who does not vary his/her usage according to situation: a native speaker who confined his usage to a single (formal) style would be unnatural and odd. All normal speakers have what is known as *communicative competence* (we elaborate further on this in Chapter 6).

  In this section, we consider restrictions imposed by prescription on the use of certain grammatical transformations. We shall be arguing that the variants actually used cannot be shown to be *ungrammatical* in any useful sense, and assuming that speakers have knowledge of what choices are appropriate and useful in varying circumstances. The sentences we shall consider can be called *topicalising* sentences containing a relative clause. Consider the simple sentence:

4 Jack built this house.

If, in a spoken context, we wish to topicalise or draw special attention to *house*, we can bring a main clause containing *house* to the front of the sentence and subordinate *Jack* in a relative clause: *that Jack built*. Thus:

5 This is the house that Jack built

or:

6 It is this house that Jack built.

Similarly, we can topicalise *Jack*:

7 It is Jack who built this house.

There are many occasions in conversation when a speaker might wish to use such devices in order to draw special attention to some person or object in the situational context or to some important topic or idea. If topicalising constructions are disallowed in some circumstances, the speaker is deprived of an important conversational strategy.

However, topicalisation of this kind is impeded under certain conditions, including the following: (a) when a possessive relative pronoun is involved: (b) when the relative clause contains an embedded indirect question. We shall discuss possessive relatives first.

Consider:

8 The roof of this house fell in.

If we topicalise *house*, we get

9 This is the house of which the roof fell in.

or

10 This is the house whose roof fell in.

Both of these seem formal and therefore tend to be avoided in informal conversational contexts: 10 might indeed be especially avoided because (even in English) speakers retain some residual feeling of grammatical gender agreement: *whose* is felt to be inappropriate with an inanimate antecedent (*house*). Topicalisation is therefore impeded, and the speaker who feels that 9 and 10 are too formal may be forced to use an avoidance strategy and revert to 8. The emphasis on *house* will then be lost, and the utterance will be deprived of the desired appropriateness to context.

Notice, however, that this is only true if we apply the requirements of *prescriptive* written grammar to speech. There are at least two ways in which spoken English can make up for the absence of a *colloquially* acceptable possessive relative. One strategy is to avoid the relative clause altogether and to use a transformation known as *left dislocation*, as in:

11 This house – its roof fell in.

The second strategy maintains the relative clause either by using a 'new' possessive: *that's*, or by using a non-possessive relative clause containing a resumptive personal pronoun, such as *its*. Examples are:

12 This is the house that's roof fell in.
13 This is the house that its roof fell in.

Sentences of this kind occur in colloquial English.

Notice that left-dislocation (as in 11) is not ungrammatical. If this term is used of left-dislocation sentences, it is being misapplied. Left-dislocation is a grammatical device of spoken English which operates in a rule-governed way on a potentially infinite number of possible sentences. We could call such a construction ungrammatical only if the transformation had been improperly carried out – if, for example, only the noun had been moved to the left, as in:

14 *House – the roof of this fell in.

When such sentences as 11 are popularly described as ungrammatical, it is meant only that the construction is felt to be inappropriate in written or formal English. The relatively narrow and well-defined norms of literary sentence construction are being improperly applied to casual speech.

Sentences 12 and 13 have in common the fact that they avoid the use of the so-called *Wh*-relative (e.g. *which*, *whose*); examples of both have been collected from informal speech in Scotland, the USA and Northern Ireland.

In 12 a new possessive relative, *that's*, has been formed to fill what speakers feel to be a gap in *colloquially* acceptable grammar. This possessive relative has been formed by a regular process (addition of the possessive inflexion -*'s*), and it refers back to *house* in precisely the same way as *of which* and *whose* do in 9 and 10. The structural difference between 12 and 9 or 10 is purely *lexical* in that a different word (*that's*) has been selected as the possessive relativiser. If 9 and 10 are grammatical, 12 is also grammatical.

The argument that 13 is ungrammatical is likely to depend on the notion of redundancy. The relative clause contains a resumptive personal pronoun *its*, which refers back to *house*, but there is already a relativiser *that*, which also refers back to *house*. Thus the pronominal function is marked twice. The resumptive pronoun is therefore said to be redundant, and the sentence may be condemned as ungrammatical, illogical or inelegant.

Arguments based on redundancy are, however, inconclusive, as all grammars of human languages contain redundancy. In English, for instance, the 3rd person verbal inflexion in *he goes* is redundant, as '3rd person' is already marked by *he*. In some languages, moreover, resumptive pronoun constructions like that of 13 are accepted in the formal literary grammar (Givón, 1979). In any case, the resumptive *its* of 13 is not wholly redundant. In addition to the pronominal function, it carries the feature 'possessive', which is absent from the relativiser *that* in 13 (but present in the relativisers of 9, 10 and 12). It is possible to regard *its* in this case simply as a necessary possessive marker.

Why, then, are 12 and 13 felt to be 'unacceptable'? The answer must clearly be connected with the ideology of standardisation, which requires uniquely 'correct' forms and characteristically uses the written channel as a model for 'correct' speech. Swift (1712) said that it was better that a language should be fixed in an imperfect state than that it should be perpetually changing: sentences 12 and 13 represent innovations in the *spoken* language (if it is measured against writing), and so the ideology of standardisation resists these innovations. The 'imperfection' in the language that these usages try to put right is the absence of *colloquially* acceptable possessive relativisers from the language. Without these relativisers, it is rather difficult to carry out certain topicalising transformations in casual speech. The effect of prescriptivism in some cases may therefore be to inhibit appropriateness in speech by reducing the range of variants available to the speaker in varying situational contexts.

We now turn to topicalised sentences in which the relative clause itself contains an embedded indirect question clause or (sometimes) a conditional clause (introduced by *when, what, where, whether, if,* etc.). In this construction, even greater difficulties occur if we prohibit resumptive pronouns.

Consider:

15 I don't know whether Jack built this house.

The noun *house* is the *object* of an embedded clause beginning with *whether* (or potentially with *when, where, how* etc.). If we topicalise *house*, we get:

16 *This is the house that I don't know whether Jack built.

This sentence is odd and would certainly be avoided both in speech and writing. Modern syntactic theory would probably conclude that a constraint has been violated in 16. Yet, if we apply the norms of *traditional* prescriptive grammar, it is difficult to show that it has been incorrectly formed: the main points are that *house* has been correctly deleted from its original clause and raised to the front of the sentence, and the relativiser *that* has been correctly supplied. What speakers *actually* do in such sentences, however, is to supply an 'incorrect' resumptive pronoun (*it*) in the slot vacated by *this house*, as follows:

17 This is the house that I don't know whether Jack built it.

The problem becomes more acute if we topicalise the *subject* of the embedded clause rather than the object, e.g.

18 *This is Jack that I don't know whether built the house.

A number of such topicalised sentences (in educated and uneducated speech) have been collected, all containing a resumptive pronoun (unlike 18). The following is typical:

19 These are the houses that we didn't know what they were like inside.

This is based on:

20 We didn't know what these houses were like inside.

'Correct' topicalisation would produce the impossible sentence:

21 *These are the houses that we didn't know what were like inside.

Sentence types such as 19 (containing the 'redundant' resumptive pronoun), however, would certainly be replaced in *written* English by some alternative construction.

It is not appropriate at this point to enter into advanced arguments about grammatical theory, such as those concerning the existence of constraints or conditions that block certain transformations (for a relevant discussion, see Radford, 1981). Although we are concerned here with traditional prescriptive grammar, we note in passing that an early version of transformational grammar might have regarded 19 as ungrammatical, on the grounds that this kind of sentence is a 'performance error': when the speaker decides to topicalise it can be said that he has not worked out how he is going to construct the rest of the sentence; an ungrammatical sentence is then said to be produced as a result of the limitations of human psychology and memory. We do not think that such sentences can actually be proved to be ungrammatical.

What is certainly clear is that sentences such as 19 do not occur in careful literary prose. Their alleged ungrammaticality seems to us to be directly due to this fact. When such sentences are judged to be ungrammatical, the norms of careful written prose (which is *planned* discourse) are being misapplied to conversational speech (*unplanned* discourse, on which see chapter 7 below), and we are again observing a malfunction of the standard ideology.

We have discussed examples of relative clause constructions in order to draw attention to some aspects of the norms of speech that differentiate it from the norms of written language. There are, of course, other syntactic differences, most of them arising from the fact that conversational speech is context-tied, whereas writing is, to a greater extent, independent of immediate situational context. Spoken language particularly needs grammatical devices for pointing to things in the surroundings in which the conversation takes place – for topicalising and giving prominence – and it has to be possible for speakers to utilise these devices rapidly. Frequently, of course, it is a matter of probability: some grammars can be used in *both* spoken and written channels, but are more *frequently* used in one channel or the other. In other cases, spoken grammars can be looked on as *extensions* of written grammars (in speech variability is functional, and linguistic change is always in progress). Whereas writing places tight restrictions on the occurrence of certain phrasal and lexical sub-types in particular constructions, spoken grammar is more 'permissive'. In the following sentences, for example, adverbials occur in subject position in all four (in broad terms their grammar is the same): yet, only the first is likely to occur in written prose (as distinct from dialogue). Example 35 is a rather memorable utterance collected during fieldwork in Belfast, in which an adverbial phrase of place appears as the subject (this sentence type is not uncommon in speech):

32 Tomorrow will be better.
33 In the morning will be better.
34 Under the table will be better.
35 Down the backstreets is more middle class.

In 32 the adverbial of time is a single word; in 33 it is a phrase; and in 34 and 35 the grammar is *extended* to admit an adverbial phrase of *place*, rather than time.

The prescriptive tradition has then imposed a narrow definition on grammaticality, very largely in the interests of developing norms of clear and unambiguous prose-writing, and it is certainly arguable that such restrictions are necessary to avoid undue ambiguity or vagueness. As the written channel is not subject to feedback and clarification processes that occur in face-to-face interaction, miscommunications cannot be repaired. Similarly, the principle of economy requires that written language should avoid undue syntactic redundancy. Speech, on the other hand, may actually *require* some redundancy so that there will be less danger of a spoken message being mis-heard. Speech can additionally tolerate regular elliptical constructions that are less common in writing. This is because speech is context-tied, and omissions can be supplied from the context; and, as we have seen, speech may also require more frequent use of devices that give prominence to certain parts of the message. For the most part, the strategies of spoken language cannot be shown to be strictly ungrammatical (see, however, the arguments of Givón, 1979); if the prescriptive grammarian resorts to the argument that they are nevertheless awkward, inelegant or vague, he appears to be saying no more than that they are unacceptable in writing. We can reply that 'to talk like a book' is equally unacceptable in casual conversational English.

In addition to influencing our ideas of what is grammatical, the prescriptive tradition (as we have seen) helps to maintain the ideology of language standardisation; standardisation aims to promote uniformity. The principle of uniformity is applied not only to spelling and morphological forms, but also to syntax and the forms and meanings of words, e.g. some constructions may be selected as 'correct' and other allegedly equivalent ones denounced as 'incorrect'. The narrow and uncritical imposition of unnecessary and inappropriate restrictions can be seen as one of the diseases or malfunctions of standardisation: another of these diseases is to extend these restrictions from written and formal ('planned') discourse to casual and informal ('unplanned') discourse. In its less critical manifestations (as in some Type 1 complaints discussed in 2.2), the prescriptive tradition has fostered in the public mind a deep ignorance of the nature of human language. As we shall see in Chapter 8, this lack of knowledge may have unfortunate consequences in practical matters: e.g. in the validity of judgments made on the basis of some language assessment procedures.

In later chapters, we shall also look at the range of skills that speakers possess in using the spoken language in varying contexts. Meantime, we extend the discussion of the grammar of speech, to consider some aspects of the grammar of varieties of English that are usually described as 'non-standard'.

4.4 The grammar of Non-Standard English

Most of the examples of spoken usage discussed in Section 4.3 can occur in the speech of persons who are judged to speak Standard English, even though they may be more common in speakers who are relatively less conscious of literary norms. In this section, we focus on usages that are more obviously non-standard.

It is important for two major reasons that the grammar of Non-Standard English should be discussed. First, many Non-Standard usages are stigmatised much more overtly and consciously than the examples of colloquial grammar discussed in 3.4, and they are usually said to be simply 'ungrammatical'. This plainly has social consequences, as the stigmatised forms are more commonly used by people in lower social groups. Stigmatisation of non-standard forms arises from a misconception as to the nature of grammaticality: what these judgments are really addressing is the notion of *acceptability*. Non-standard usages of certain kinds are simply not socially 'acceptable' in formal and high status contexts. They are stereotyped markers of social class and/or casual style. Second, the persistence of non-standard usages (which are allegedly ungrammatical) is commonly thought to arise from ignorance, incompetence or even cognitive deficiency on the part of speakers. Non-standard speakers are thought to be either perversely unwilling or mentally incapable of acquiring the 'superior' norms of 'correct' English. As the consequences of such attitudes can be serious (e.g. judgments made on the abilities of children at school), it is important that we establish that non-standard varieties are in themselves grammatical and rule-governed forms of English. We shall confine our discussion in this section to the grammar (syntax and morphology) of NSE; pronunciation of NSE will be discussed in Chapter 5.

Much of the syntax of non-standard English is actually the same as that of the standard. All varieties have a generalised SVO word-order; thus, *John likes coffee* is grammatical, and **John coffee likes* is ungrammatical in all varieties of spoken English. All English dialects are prepositional, not postpositional: **the house in* is ungrammatical in all varieties. Similarly, many of the rules for *ellipsis* are common to all dialects: for instance, no British dialect (as far as we know) regularly permits deletion of the object in a prepositional phrase. In spoken standard Danish *Tag kager hjem med* ('take cakes home with') is grammatical: in all varieties of English, however, the object of the preposition is supplied, as in 'Take cakes home with you'. A rare exception to this is the expression: 'Are you coming with?'. This seems to be restricted to the verb: *come*, and the preposition: *with*, and possibly only to second person address (***John came with yesterday' does not seem possible). In Danish, and other Germanic languages, the objectless preposition is very widely distributed.

In some ways, however, the syntax and morphology of non-standard varieties differ from Standard English. Some of these differences are relatively superficial: they involve alternative forms for grammatical connectors (conjunctions, prepositions, relativisers and complementisers) without necessarily affecting syntax and meaning; they also involve particular word-forms that are chosen to express verb-tenses (such as *seen* for *saw*) and inflexional differences (such as *he don't* for *he doesn't*). It is these superficial differences of word-form that are particularly noticed and stigmatised (as in the letter from 'Have Went' quoted in Chapter 2). Indeed, as we shall see in Chapter 8, it is often superficial differences of this kind that language assessment procedures identify, rather than more important linguistic problems. There are, however, some deeper and more thorough-going differences between dialects that are of a syntactic kind, involving varying conventions of word-order and tense/aspect differences in the verḃal system. These latter differences are great enough to suggest that underlying semantic structures are different; but, important as these are, they attract much less public notice than do the superficial differences. In what follows, we discuss some superficial differences first. We start with *connectors* and follow with *verb morphology*.

4.4.1   Connectors

In English speech there is a good deal of variation in the choice of connecting particles (conjunctions, prepositions) and relativisers. In Northern English, *while* is equivalent to 'until' in e.g. *Wait while six o'clock*. In Northern Irish English, *whenever* can be equivalent to *when*: thus, *whenever George VI was King*, does *not* mean 'on every occasion that George VI was King'. This usage arises from a difference in word-selection in temporal clauses and from an underlying difference in the grammatical system of temporal connectors as between Northern Irish English and SE.

Many of these variations are best described as lexical rather than syntactic. Some NSE varieties, for example, use *what* or *as* as relativisers in preference to *who/which*, as in:

1 This is a boy what loves his mother.
2 This is a boy as loves his mother.

The *what* and *as* clauses are relative clauses, and the non-standard speaker is no less capable of constructing a relative clause than the standard speaker: the difference is in the lexical items chosen as relativisers. We can think of the standard speaker as having in his head a list of items (*who, which, that*...) which function as relativisers, and of non-standard speakers as having a list that is partly or wholly different. Many speakers may indeed have the capacity to vary between standard and non-standard usages on different occasions, according to what is felt appropriate in varying circumstances. The idea that the use of stigmatised forms is a sign of ignorance or backwardness is particularly hard to accept when we consider this capacity of speakers to vary (i.e. their *communicative competence*, as discussed in Chapter 6).

It is an accident of history that SE, and not certain other dialects, has fixed on *who/which* rather than *what* as relativisers. Latin could use *quod* (the equivalent of *what*) as a relativiser, and standard German permits *was* ('what') in the same capacity. Similarly, some standard languages use the equivalent of *as*. In Danish *som Du vil* means 'as you wish': *som* ('as') is also used as a relativiser, as in *det store hus som jeg så i dag*: (lit.) 'the big house as I saw today'.

4.4.2 *Verb morphology and concord*

So-called misuses of verb-forms, as in *I does, I seen it*, are particularly salient features of non-standard English. Like the use of *what, as* as relativisers, these non-standard verb forms are social class markers, and many have particular regional distributions: *I does* is not found in certain northern varieties, and many southern varieties prefer *I see it* to *I seen it* as a past tense. In general, non-standard varieties, when compared with the standard, have a compulsion to simplify (to eliminate differences such as *saw* (past tense) v. *seen* (past participle)) and regularise: in so doing they reduce what we have called redundant distinctions and move in the direction of greater *transparency*.

A typical non-standard present tense paradigm is (cf. Cheshire, 1982a):

I goes	we goes
you goes	you goes
he goes	they goes

Typical simplifications of past tense/past participle are represented by:

see:	(I) seen	(I have) seen
do:	(I) done	(I have) done
come:	(I) come	(I have) come

The above generalise the participle form to the past tense. In some verbs the 'original' past tense form is generalised to the participle, as in:

take:	(I) took	(I have) took
go:	(I) went	(I have) went

Many of these simplifications are extremely widespread throughout the English-speaking world. The distinctions that are obliterated by these simplifications are redundant. There is no loss of communicative efficiency in the choice of *I have took* as against *I have taken*. 'Perfect tense' is adequately marked by the auxiliary *have*. Nor does choice of the non-standard form indicate that the speaker does not *know* the difference between past and perfect tenses: he has merely chosen a different (regularised) form of the verb to express past or perfective tense/aspect. In non-standard uses, these irregular verbs have become regularised in order to fit in with the general pattern of English verbs (in which past tense and participle are not distinguished), as in:

walk:	(I) walked	(I have) walked
wonder:	(I) wonder	(I have) wondered

Historically, these simplifications are of the greatest interest. Since Old English times, the language has been losing its inflexional apparatus, and the spoken language (especially in NSE) has continued this trend. The written language, however, has been standardised in a form that maintains certain traditional formal distinctions in irregular verbs.

It appears that the eighteenth-century prescriptive grammarians were responsible for 'legitimising' many of these distinctions (such as *saw* v. *seen*). They may well have been on the point of disappearing from the language. Long before – around 1600 – Shakespeare had often failed to make formal distinctions between past tense and past participle – even in speeches by high-status characters in blank verse, e.g.,

'I have already chose my officer' (*Othello* 1, i) or
'The King himself is rode to view their battle' (*Henry V* 4, iii).

Prescriptive authorities are usually conservative in that they are inclined to prefer older usages. In helping to preserve the irregular verbs of English, the eighteenth-century grammarians were also influenced by their admiration for Latin (which is highly inflected), and they were inclined to preserve tense, number and person distinctions as much as they could, on the model of Latin. We can attribute the relative conservatism of SE in this respect to the standard ideology in the shape of eighteenth-century prescriptivism. NSE varieties have continued to do without redundant distinctions; 'incorrect' regularisation of verb-forms has become stigmatised by the standard ideology, and the 'correct' irregular forms are prescribed in the writing system.

The prescriptive ideology can insist on maintaining morphological distinctions that are of doubtful utility, while at the same time resisting potentially useful innovations in colloquial forms. NSE dialects do not simplify in all respects: the introduction of new 2nd person plural pronouns (such as *yous* and *y'all*) adds a potentially useful distinction to the grammar; yet it is stigmatised. Similarly, the lack of an epicene (masculine and feminine) pronoun in English is often felt to be inconvenient: colloquial speech often uses *they* in this function, but the narrower forms of prescription reject this and enjoin us to say, for example, *When everyone has finished eating, would he or she please put away his or her plate?*

There are many interesting features of non-standard morphology that we have no space to discuss. However, before we go on to discuss some deeper syntactic differences that suggest that the underlying structure (not merely the superficial forms) of some dialects is different from SE, we shall briefly consider a concord-rule found in some Scots and Northern Irish vernacular speech.

In N. Irish English (as in many other regional forms) the following construction is regular:

1 The houses is nice

A plural noun phrase does not require the selection of the SE plural form of the verb *to be*. We might therefore suppose that,

2 *They is nice

is also grammatical in the dialect. However, the dialect requires the form *are* following plural personal pronouns (and 2nd person singular), and 2 is ungrammatical. In short, while the dialect grammar appears to be simpler than SE in one respect, it is more complicated in another. An outsider learning the dialect must learn to make a distinction between the concord rules for noun-phrases and those for personal pronouns. Non-native speakers of the dialect plainly have no intuitions about this grammar: in a television production of Gerald Seymour's novel, *Harry's Game* (shown in 1982 and 1983), an alleged Northern Irish speaker was made to say:

3 *He's a hard man, but so is you, Billy.

So is you is impossible in N. Irish speech.

Non-standard grammars are, therefore, not merely simplified and inaccurate versions of SE. They have their own histories, their own rules and their own structures. Some aspects of them have been discussed by Labov 1972b, 1972c, and Trudgill, Edwards and Weltens, 1982, but in general we know far less about them than we should. As we shall see in Chapter 8, the practical importance of this general ignorance for language assessment procedures should not be underestimated.

4.4.3 *Deeper grammatical differences in NSE*

Syntactic differences in different varieties of English range in depth from fairly superficial word-order differences ('He gave me it' *v.* 'He gave it me') to very subtle differences of syntactic choice in the verb system, for the expression of tense and aspect distinctions. These differences suggest that there are differences in semantic structure; certainly, the semantic area divided between SE past and perfect tenses is not divided in the same way in all other dialects. From a historical point of view, it should not be surprising that tense/aspect differences should exist: in Old English, the perfect tense (as in *I have done it*) seems to have been poorly developed, and progressive aspect (as in *I am doing it*) does not seem to have been fully incorporated into the verb system until quite recently (see Traugott, 1972 for a historical account of the English verb system). The English verb system is so complicated, and that of SE so different from that of early English, that we should expect modern varieties to have preserved some usages obsolete in SE, or to have developed independently. In what follows, we shall briefly mention progressive and habitual aspect and give fuller consideration to perfective aspect.

In SE, certain 'private state' verbs (*like, want*, etc.) do not usually occur in the progressive form (unlike 'dynamic' verbs such as *hit, push*): in some dialects, however, use of the progressive extends to some of these verbs, as in:

4 He's wanting it.
5 I'm not caring.

These usages seem to be preferred in Scottish and Irish English.

The tense/aspect system of non-standard Hiberno-English is radically different from that of SE. This is often attributed to the influence of Irish Gaelic; yet some of the features of the system also appear to have models in older English (Harris, 1982, 1984). The origin of the system is mixed.

Hiberno-English (like many English-based creoles) makes a distinction between *punctual* and *habitual* aspect by selecting different forms of the verb *to be*, as in:

6 He is there (at this moment): punctual;
7 He does be there (every day): habitual.

Thus, these varieties have a grammatical resource not available in SE.

The most thoroughgoing difference, however, is in the selection of forms that express perfective aspect (i.e. reference to something happening in the past which retains current relevance). Some Hiberno-English dialects simply do not have forms like 'He *has done* it': they can express the same (or similar) meaning, but they do it in different ways.

In some circumstances, the *present* tense is used, as in:

8 How long are you here?

In SE this means either 'How long will you be here? or 'What is the total length of your stay?' In Hib-E, it means 'How long *have you been* here?', and the appropriate reply might well be: 'I'm here since Tuesday'.

In other circumstances, the simple past tense is used. Thus in Hib-E (together with most Scottish and American English) the past tense form can collocate with adverbs like *yet*, *already*, as in:

9 Did you have your dinner yet?

To this, an appropriate response might be:

10 Yes, I had it already.

(These collocations are reported to be prevented in SE, which is said to require perfect tense with *yet*, *already*.)

If the Hib-E speaker wishes to refer to an activity that has taken place a short time before, he can use a periphrastic construction literally translated from Irish Gaelic:

11 John is after eating his dinner.
12 John is after his dinner.

This expression means that John has had his dinner recently, *not* that he is looking for his dinner (as it would be interpreted in SE).

Yet another construction is preferred when an activity occupying a period of time has come to an end: this has a different word-order from the SE perfect construction. An example is:

13 John has his dinner eaten.

Notice that this construction is unlikely to be used when the verb involved is one of momentary activity, possibly for the reason that the activity referred to has to have some duration (but see Harris, 1984). Thus,

14 John has the ball kicked

is unlikely to occur because the act of kicking has little duration. This means that the Hiberno-English perfective system does not match up exactly with SE, in that we cannot simply 'translate' *John has kicked the ball* as *John has the ball kicked*. It obviously differs in quite a deep-rooted way, and at first sight it appears to be more complicated. In writing a full grammar of this variety of English we should have to specify quite a different set of patterns and choices than those that are specified in accounts of the Standard English verb (e.g. Palmer, 1965).

4.5   Conclusions

Traditionally, judgments about grammaticality have been based on the codified norms of written English, and in this chapter we have called attention to the inappropriateness of many prescriptive judgments of spoken English that are made on this basis. In the experience of the individual, speech is prior to writing: the English grammar that the child learns is the grammar of speech, and this is correctly named 'grammar' whether the variety acquired is 'standard' or 'non-standard'. A sequence like *the man what I saw* is not *ungrammatical* in some non-standard variety: it is merely *unacceptable* in writing, in standardised speech, and in some formal registers of speech.

It has for some centuries been relatively easy to judge grammaticality as if it were a property of the written channel, for the reason that written norms have been codified whereas the norms of speech have not. The functions of speech are, however, so varied and so different from those of writing that such judgments are often inappropriate and can be damaging if they are taken too seriously. The variability of speech is a resource exploited by speakers to mark differences in conversational styles and appropriateness to varying situational contexts. In some such contexts (e.g. in some industrial contexts such as coal-mines in Yorkshire), literary grammar is hardly appropriate or functional, and non-standard grammar is preferred – or even enforced.

In the next two chapters, we extend the discussion to pronunciation differences and focus more fully on an issue we have raised in this chapter – *communicative competence*. This notion attempts to account for the capacity of speakers to vary their speech according to social and situational contexts.

5
Linguistic prescription and the speech community

5.1 Introduction

Thus far, we have considered prescriptive attitudes to correctness as arising from an ideology of language standardisation, and have noted that these prescriptive attitudes are therefore social, rather than strictly linguistic in nature. Structural differences between varieties of a language are, from a purely linguistic point of view, neutral and arbitrary.

In fact, as we have tried to demonstrate in Chapter 2 (using English as the language of exemplification), relatively trivial linguistic differences are frequently seized upon and magnified, forming in due course the subject matter of a distinct *complaint tradition*. This happens quite consistently in technologically advanced societies which require a heavily codified standard language, and indeed one of the functions of linguistic complaint is the promotion of that standard. A further effect (which we have not yet discussed in detail) is the development of a linguistic value system which both reflects and reinforces social class and power distinctions (see Sankoff, 1980 for an account of the recent emergence of such a value system in Papua New Guinea). Generally, people are acutely aware of the social effects of this value system, and educators are particularly sensitive to the pressures it exerts in the form of requirements that all pupils should be able to write, and if possible speak, Standard English.

In this chapter we look more closely at the manifestations of the value system, and adopt two different perspectives. First, we look at the distribution of socially sensitive linguistic elements in some real speech communities. This section may be seen as complementing the structural account of non-standard English syntax and morphology in Chapter 4; we concentrate here, by way of contrast, on *phonology* (including non-standard phonological elements) which for reasons which will become clear is best described *quantitatively* where the objective is to compare differences in language use by different sections of the community.

Second, we assess some specifically prescriptive comments on the linguistic adequacy of those same phonological elements. As we have already noted in connection with the English complaint tradition, these more specific prescriptive comments are more easily interpreted in terms of the value system than in terms of their linguistic accuracy. We then go on to consider some effects of prescriptivism in educational systems.

In recent years, quantitative methods of description and analysis have resulted in considerable advances in our detailed under-standing of the relationship between linguistic choice and various social characteristics of the speaker. Although some quantitative studies have become well known in educational circles, we do not assume that readers are necessarily familiar with either the techniques or the findings associated with them. Thus, the major relevant issues are discussed here.

As early as 1958, John Fischer studied the way in which 24 children in a New England village varied between the [ɪn] and the [ɪŋ] pronunciations of the present participle, in words like *running, coming, going*. We shall refer to these informally as the *-in'* and *-ing* pronunciations. What interested Fischer was that most of the children seemed to use *both* forms, rather than either one or the other. However, if enough instances of the present participle were observed for each child, it emerged that the children mixed the *-in'* and the *-ing* forms in different proportions. Briefly, girls were much more likely to use the *-ing* forms than boys; boys described by the teacher as 'model' boys (i.e. those whose behaviour was good) were more likely to use the *-ing* form than 'typical' mischievous boys, and choice of *-ing* rather than *-in'* was more likely if the child's family was of relatively high status or if the interview during which speech was tape-recorded was manipulated so as to be relatively formal. Thus, at least one linguistic element which is traditionally subject to classroom correction (the present participle ending) appears to be used in different ways according to a number of factors (such as sex, personality and family) which are quite outside the teacher's control.

Quantitative techniques of analysis – that is, those which view use of elements such as *-in'* as opposed to *-ing* as a matter of *greater* or *less*, rather than as *absolute* patterns of use – were more fully developed by William Labov. In 1966, Labov published his famous study of five linguistic variables in the Lower East Side of New York City. A linguistic variable is defined as a linguistic element which appears in different forms (or variants) in the speech community. Thus, the *-in'* and *-ing* variants of the present participle studied by Fischer are good examples of variants of a single underlying variable. However, Labov developed more sophisticated techniques for dealing with large numbers of linguistic instances (or tokens) of these variables. His basic method was to calculate a linguistic *score* for a given speaker or a given social group. This score expresses the *actual use* of a linguistic variant as a proportion of its *maximum possible* use. Thus, if we were studying a speaker's use of the present participle, we would not simply count the number of times he said *-ing* rather than *-in'*. Rather, we would consider both *-in'* and *-ing* as representing an occasion when either variant *could* have been chosen and we would relate the number of occurrences of *-ing* proportionately to the speaker's total use of both *-in'* and *-ing*. The detailed scores which appear in Tables 5.1, 5.2 and 5.3 below are examples of the kind of figure which emerge from this quantitative technique of analysis. If the variable is considered to have only two variants (like the *-ing/-in'* example), the speaker's score is expressed as a percentage; relatively simple binary variables of this kind are all that we need to consider in this book. The advantage of this kind of analysis is that it allows the language of different speakers (or of the same speaker on different occasions) to be compared in a systematic manner, so that general facts about language use in the community emerge fairly clearly.

After language use has been analysed in this way, scores may be examined for correspondence with extra-linguistic variables such as the status, age and sex of the speaker, or the relative formality of the situation. There is a good deal of controversy surrounding the manner in which some extra-linguistic variables are defined and measured. For example, although sex and age are usually unproblematic, class and status are social constructs which mean something quite different to different social theorists. However, linguists have, on the whole, been involved in unravelling technical *linguistic* complexities (which are not relevant here) and have tended to avoid becoming enmeshed in sociological controversies. Generally, a social class index, usually based on occupation, education, residence and income, is used simply as a convenient way of making some sense of the distribution of linguistic variation. One advance which we might expect to see in the future is a greater sociological sophistication in the handling of the crucial variable of social class.

5.2   The social distribution of linguistic variants

Following these introductory remarks, we look now at some quantitative data which have been calculated in the manner described in the previous section, and which reveal the systematic relationship between language use and various social factors. All the linguistic variables discussed in this section have been chosen because they are well known targets of adverse comment and have, in fact, been mentioned briefly in previous chapters.

The dropping of [h] in England, the use of the glottal stop in Scotland, and the choice of -*in'* rather than -*ing* in English-speaking communities generally, have all been described variously as sloppy, lazy, ugly or incoherent. Table 5.1 shows the incidence of [h]-dropping according to social class in two English cities, Bradford and Norwich; the figures refer to the relatively careful style of speech used during tape-recorded interviews (see p. 94 below). However, it is worth remembering that we are discussing [h]-dropping in *stressed* syllables only; all speakers of English drop [h] regularly in unstressed positions. An example of this very general [h]-dropping, which is not very obvious to listeners, is the pronunciation of the personal pronoun *him* as in 'JOHN saw him THEN' where both *John* and *then* are accented. Thus, quite apart from the patterns revealed in Table 5.1, [h]-dropping occurs regularly in English in specific linguistic contexts, in even the most careful, educated speech.

It is clear, as we might expect, that in both Bradford and Norwich, speakers of relatively high status show a progressive tendency to approximate to the spoken standard of Received Pronunciation, which does not drop [h] in stressed syllables. Another point is that there is a certain amount of [h]-dropping amongst even the highest status groups studied in the two cities. Thus, although [h]-dropping is socially stigmatised, it is a community norm which quite simply affects to some extent the speech of all social groups. This is not surprising if we remember that [h]-dropping has been an active sociolinguistic process in English for a very long time (see p. 20 above) and may even at some point

Table 5.1   Percentage of [h]*-dropping in Bradford and Norwich (formal style)*

	Bradford	Norwich
Middle middle class	12	6
Lower middle class	28	14
Upper working class	67	40
Middle working class	89	60
Lower working class	93	60

(After Chambers and Trudgill, 1980:69 and Petyt, 1977.)

have been prestigious. We see also that [h]-dropping is more common in Bradford than in Norwich amongst *all* social groups, although it shows a decrease with increasing status in exactly the same way in both cities. This difference in absolute level of use is probably in some part a reflection of the fact that [h]-dropping is not a regionally distributed characteristic of the rural speech of East Anglia, with which the urban dialect of Norwich has affinities, while rural Yorkshire speech *is* characterised by [h]-dropping.

The general social sensitivity of speakers to variables such as these may be shown by examining their distribution according to style. Table 5.2 illustrates this point, with reference once more to the present participle. The incidence of *-in'* as opposed to *-ing* in Norwich is shown (in such words as *running, jumping*) according to whether the speaker is (a) reading word lists and might therefore be expected to pay careful attention to each word; (b) reading a passage of connected prose – a slightly less careful style; (c) responding to direct questions in a tape-recorded interview and therefore

Table 5.2   Percentage of -in' *in Norwich, shown according to style and class*

	WLS	RPS	FS	CS
Middle middle class	0	0	3	28
Lower working class	0	10	15	42
Upper working class	5	15	74	87
Middle working class	23	44	88	95
Lower working class	29	66	98	100

(After Chambers and Trudgill, 1980: 71.)

speaking fairly self-consciously but paying less attention to his speech than he would to a reading task; or (d) talking relatively casually when his attention has been diverted away from the fact that his speech is being tape-recorded. Thus, the four styles WLS (word-list-style), RPS (reading passage style), FS (formal style) and CS (casual style) may be interpreted as a continuum along which speakers move as they pay progressively less attention to producing careful speech.

The striking feature of this array (and one which is very relevant to anyone who is trying to modify a speaker's language patterns) is its total consistency. Scores increase regularly across rows and down columns, showing that although social groups characteristically use different levels of *-in'*, they all agree in style shifting in the same direction as their speech style alters on the dimension of formality. One major question of interest, particularly to teachers who want their pupils to be able to control the standard form of language, is *why* people such as those in the lowest status group continue to use stigmatised elements like *-in'* when data such as those in Table 5.2 clearly reveal both their sensitivity to this variable and the fact that they are able to adjust its frequency quite considerably in formal contexts. In fact, their usage in formal contexts approximates quantitatively to the casual norm of the *highest* social group. An answer to this question (to which we will later give some attention) would seem to be of importance to an understanding of why adverse comments on the use of variants like *-in'* (and, by implication, other socially distributed variants) frequently seem to be ineffective. Meantime, we complete our examination of quantitatively analysed patterns of variation by looking at the distribution of two variants of the present participle, this time with attention to both the *sex* and the *social class* of the speaker.

Again, as in Table 5.2, the pattern is extremely consistent. Women in each social group approximate more closely than men to the publicly legitimized norm, a tendency which has been confirmed in many studies of different speech communities. A number of explanations of these sex-based patterns have been proposed, which need not concern us here. However, what is important is that the general patterns shown by Tables 5.1, 5.2 and 5.3 have been repeated in surveys other than those in Bradford and Norwich. They emerge not only for a large number of linguistic variables in Britain and America, but in sociolinguistic surveys of other languages such as the Canadian French of Montreal and the Persian

Table 5.3   -in' *in Norwich, according to sex*
and social class of speaker

	Total	Male	Female
Middle middle class	3	4	0
Lower middle class	15	27	3
Upper working class	74	81	68
Middle working class	88	91	81
Lower working class	98	100	97

of (pre-revolution) Tehran. Generally speaking, higher social groups approximate increasingly more closely to high prestige norms, and women approximate more closely than men to the same norms. All speakers appear to vary their language according to stylistic context, so showing their sensitivity to these same variables. Moreover, it appears from a number of recent studies of young children that linguistic sex-grading and style-shifting are already well established long before children leave primary school. The general picture from a very early age is thus one of relatively low level linguistic elements being intertwined quite inextricably with social distinctions of various kinds important in the community. This intimate and extremely consistent connection between social and linguistic structure appears to have the effect of making speakers very resistant to attempts to change their language patterns.

As we noted in Chapters 1 and 2 (pp. 16–36), social structure takes hold of language variation in an *arbitrary* manner. Pronunciations like *comin'* and *goin'* have not always been associated with low status speech as is shown in Tables 5.2 and 5.3. Dorothy L. Sayers's orthographic representation of the speech of Lord Peter Wimsey suggests that this linguistic element was quite stereotypical of upper-class speech in the early years of the twentieth century and, indeed, older upper-class speakers can still be heard using the *in'* variant occasionally. However, the social evaluation accorded to *in'* has altered, as it appears no longer to be generally characteristic of upper-class British speakers.

The arbitrary character of socially sensitive linguistic variables is also shown if we consider [h]-dropping (see also Chapter 2); [h]-dropping appears to be socially very important in England as far north as County Durham, but is in fact irrelevant in cities such as Newcastle, Glasgow or Belfast where it is not characteristic of the dialect at all. The fact is that neither working class nor any other native speakers drop [h] in those areas. The same arbitrariness is shown in the United States, where the presence of postvocalic [r] in words like *car* and *cart* has changed within living memory from a marker of low prestige to one of high prestige. In England, the opposite evaluation applies, while Scotland and Ireland are different again.

5.3 Some common prescriptions: a critique

So far, we have noted the extremely regular distribution through communities of stigmatised linguistic variants like the zero form of (h) and the *-in'* form of (ng). If we bear in mind the consistency of these patterns, the generality of the stigma attached to them is striking. We move on now to examine, in relation to this consistency, some prescriptive comments and their implications.

First of all, it is clearly the language habits associated most strongly with male speakers and working-class speakers which are stigmatised. It has already been emphasised that there is no obvious *linguistic* reason for this stigma; working-class dialects operate within working-class communities as efficiently as any other linguistic system, sometimes including useful distinctions which are not present in the standard forms of the language. As we have already noted, the distinction in Belfast and Glasgow between *you* (singular) and *yous* (plural) is a good example of this (see p. 14 above); yet Belfast working-class speech, like the working-class speech of other cities, is still widely considered both by the general public, and by teachers and employers, to be ugly, lazy and generally inadequate. Since we are attempting to examine the nature and effects of prescriptivism, it is important for at least two reasons to emphasize the absence of linguistic realism from many prescriptive comments.

First, prescriptivism in its extreme and illiberal form (which, in our terms is usually a manifestation of a Type 1 complaint) amounts to a rejection of the social values of the speaker; many teachers are worried about the implications of rejecting speakers in this way under cover of their roles as educators. The counterproductive nature of prescriptive attitudes (and of feelings of guilt about such attitudes) in the classroom, and their damaging effect on good and systematic English teaching (as well as the teaching of other subjects), has been discussed in detail by Halliday, McIntosh and Strevens (1964:75–111, 232–52, and more recently by Trudgill (1975) and Cheshire (1982b). Since many critics of prescriptivism are keenly aware of the need for good English teaching, an awareness of the social implications of prescriptivism does not amount, as is sometimes assumed, to the abandonment of any attempt to teach Standard English.

On the contrary, as Cheshire's study of teachers' strategies for correcting the 'mistakes' of non-standard speakers makes clear, Standard English cannot be taught efficiently unless the teacher has a clear understanding of the small, but systematic, differences between Standard English and the non-standard dialect of his pupils. If every expression which does not correspond to Standard English is counted as a 'mistake', and if non-standard constructions are not differentiated from 'genuine' mistakes, pupils become unnecessarily confused. Cheshire has demonstrated in detail how this confusion affects the written work of pupils, and has argued convincingly that an important prerequisite to effective teaching is an awareness of the grammatical structure of the local dialect (which differs in only a small number of relatively superficial ways from Standard English). Similarly, Gannon (1982) and Sinclair (1982) argue for a careful analytic approach to English language teaching, based on sound linguistic principles.

There is a second practical reason for us to emphasise the lack of linguistic realism in most prescriptive comment. Persons in positions of authority are often prepared to be openly critical of a speaker's language when they would not be prepared to reject publicly other aspects of his identity or culture. Yet as Halliday *et al.* point out,

> A speaker who is made ashamed of his own language habits suffers a basic injury as a human being: to make anyone, especially a child, feel so ashamed is as indefensible as to make him feel ashamed of the colour of his skin. (1964:105)

The transcripts provided by Macaulay (1977) of the linguistic views of people in Glasgow such as employers, teachers and lecturers illustrate this point very clearly, in that they reveal a sharp disjunction between overtly sympathetic attitudes to disadvantaged

Glasgow people, and an equally overt stigmatisation of 'broad' Glasgow speech. But if we thoroughly grasp that the underlying logic of prescriptivism is social rather than linguistic, we must take the view that prescriptive comments on linguistic correctness amount to an indirect expression of a social prejudice which cannot acceptably be directly expressed.

For these two reasons, it is valuable to recognise and discuss openly not only the social (as opposed to linguistic) motives underlying prescriptivism, but also its positive social function as a mechanism for maintaining the standard norm. If these important functional aspects of prescriptivism are recognised as such, rather than expressed as moral judgements concerning the 'carelessness' and 'sloppiness' of speakers, it may be possible to make some progress with such contentious problems as how Standard English might best be taught to non-standard speakers. We are not attempting in this book to give a clear set of practical recommendations (readers are referred to Carter, ed., 1982 and Cheshire, 1982b, for clear discussions of related issues as they emerge in the classroom).

What we *are* attempting is a more balanced discussion of linguistic prescriptivism within a broader social and political context than has been usual. Until such a discussion does take place, it is unlikely that related practical problems such as those of teaching non-standard speakers to write Standard English can be adequately tackled. At the moment, public discussion of this problem tends to be polarised between certain linguists who point out that prescriptive comments are linguistically unjustified, and certain educationalists who do not see the relevance of this observation to educational problems. A recent example of the inadequate level at which this important debate is sometimes pursued may be found in Honey (1983). (But see also Crystal, 1983 and Hudson, 1983 for critiques of Honey).

One effect of the paucity of meaningful debate on the nature and function of prescriptivism is that published prescriptive comments, designed to be used as linguistic guidelines by their audiences, are often misleading and inaccurate (see the discussion of Metcalfe's work on p. 72 above). That this is so even when they are formulated by persons who, unlike Metcalfe, have considerable expertise in formal linguistic analysis, may be demonstrated by examining comments in two speech training manuals on the phonological feature known as the *glottal stop*.

5.3.1   *The glottal stop*

This is an extremely well-known stereotype of urban Scottish speech which occurs between vowels and in word final positions as a variant of the consonant /t/. Thus, the phonetic sequences [bʌʔer] and [bɪʔ] (sometimes represented orthographically as *bu'er* and *bi'*) are very common pronunciations of the words *butter* and *bit*. Other examples of words where the glottal stop can appear as a variant of /t/ are *metal, Latin, cut, bought*, but not *ten, take, tiny, stop, left*.

The glottal stop receives widespread condemnation from teachers and from the public generally in Scotland. However, it also appears in educated Southern British speech in certain contexts, notably as a boundary marker between words where the second word begins with a vowel. Examples are 'an (glottal stop) apple'; 'an (glottal stop) orange'; 'these (glottal stop) arrange-ments'. Sometimes, speakers who use a glottal stop in this position hear the same phrases spoken in Scottish or Irish accents (which do not use the glottal stop in this way) as if they were 'a napple' 'a norange', 'thee zarrangements'.

When the glottal stop appears between words like this, it is not apparently subject to criticism in the same way as it is when it appears as a variant of /t/; presumably for the reason that it does not have a socially patterned distribution in this position, it attracts little attention. Since the glottal stop also appears in the standard forms of other languages (notably Danish and classical Arabic) it is hard to see any *linguistic* justification for the general condem-nation which it receives when it appears in urban Scottish speech.

One example of this specific criticism may be found in an influen-tial speech training manual, where it is held to be particularly undesirable as 'it detracts from intelligibility' (MacAllister, 1963:66). A little thought suggests that this comment should be treated with caution, since the glottal stop is restricted to limited phonetic contexts; it appears as a substitute for /t/ only between vowels and at the end of words. Of course any non-standard accent tends to be unintelligible to those unfamiliar with it. But any detraction from intelligibility resulting *directly* from the use of the glottal stop seems unlikely in view of the findings of Macaulay's survey of Glasgow speech that, on average, speakers from four social groups used the glottal stop 74 per cent of the time. Moreover, as we would expect, its use is modified (particularly by

middle-class speakers) in the careful styles appropriate to interactions with strangers who might not be familiar with the Glasgow
accent. In Glasgow itself, and in Edinburgh also, according to
Romaine & Reid (1976), it appears to be an important community
norm.

5.3.2 /t/deletion

MacAllister's manual is not the only one to criticise the glottal stop,
nor is it necessarily criticised with particular reference to Scottish
speech. For example, one text which is widely used for elocution
training in Northern Ireland (but written from the perspective of
RP), goes so far as to criticise it in the word boundary positions in
which, according to Gimson's careful account, it appears in Standard Southern British English (Luck, 1975:91). Luck is critical also
of a wide range of socially and regionally distributed linguistic
features, usually attributing to them characteristics such as laziness
and ugliness. However, as well as condemning the 'educated'
glottal stop distribution, he criticises a number of other features
which are also described in standard texts such as Gimson (1980),
Wells and Colson (1975), as occurring in educated Southern British
speech. For example, he attacks deletion of /t/ between consonants
in such phrases as 'next station' or 'last stop', where according
to Wells and Colson, deletion occurs regularly in Received
Pronunciation.

The actual facts of /t/ deletion in English have been documented
in a descriptive account of the modern spoken language, designed
principally to help foreign learners understand the forms of the
language which they hear from educated speakers such as broadcasters and university lecturers. Brown (1977) has analysed deletion
of /t/ between consonants in the speech of BBC news readers. This
can hardly be called 'rapid' or 'careless' speech, but nevertheless,
the following examples are listed as phrases where /t/ is deleted:
'firs*t* three'; las*t* year'; 'mos*t* recent'; 'interes*t* rates'; 'Wes*t*
German'; 'the fac*t* that'; 'aspec*ts*'; 'conflic*t* still'; 'mus*t* be'; 'pro-
tes*t* meeting'. The author goes on to comment:

This process [of /t/ deletion between consonants] is so common
that one is surprised to hear a /t/ in the stream of speech in this
position. In scores of examples of *West German* and *West*

Germany in my data I can find none where a medial /t/ is heard. This is a well established habit even in quite slow and deliberate speech.

(Brown, 1977:61)

In view of Brown's observations here, we may conclude that prescriptions of the kind found in Luck's manual not only are social rather than linguistic in character, but lack any standard of even limited descriptive accuracy. Thus, quite apart from the social motives underlying such comments, they can be legitimately criticised for their inaccuracy. And, as Haas (1982) has pointed out, the work of the great classical Greek grammarians has shown that linguistic prescriptions need not be descriptively inaccurate. Despite their popularity, it is hard to see how manuals such as those of Luck and MacAllister can provide a basis for teaching *any* variety of current spoken English. Yet unless a means is developed of relating facts about language use to the needs of teachers and pupils – needs which are defined at the moment mainly in terms of unworkable prescriptions – we shall continue to have only inadequate teaching materials at our disposal.

5.4   A wider perspective on prescriptivism

The points which we have been emphasising so far are chiefly concerned with the social mechanisms underlying prescriptivism, in view of the fact that the linguistic sign is arbitrary and value-free. But the very existence of these social mechanisms means that prescriptivism is an extremely sensitive (and even emotive) issue, and so is difficult to discuss in a detached manner. Moreover, many teachers, including the large number who are worried by over-prescriptive approaches in the classroom, may feel that the arguments presented here are of little use in helping them face practical problems. In fact, a start is being made on tackling these problems (see again Cheshire, 1982b; Carter, ed., 1982), but just as important as the introduction of systematic means of coping with the difficulties of non-standard speakers in the educational system is some change in prevailing attitudes to non-standard speech. Although it is likely that a more open discussion of prescriptivism and its consequences in employment, education and assessment will help to modify these attitudes, we do not think that full and open discussion of the implications of this important issue (most people would agree that it *is* important) are often to be found in print.

Sometimes, unfortunately, it is the subject of an extended debate (conducted through the columns of a newspaper) which degenerates into open expressions of ill-informed prejudice.

There is another problem in discussing prescriptivism which is harder to pin down, but which seems to be related to the social sensitivity associated with the topic. Many intelligent people appreciate and accept the arguments of linguists about the arbitrariness of linguistic signs and the adequacy of non-standard varieties as structurally (though perhaps not functionally) effective communicative systems. But even given such tolerance, it is extremely difficult for anyone to calculate the extent to which his general attitudes to language have been coloured by prevailing prescriptions. As a consequence, reactions to non-standard speech often accord with these learnt attitudes, even when at a rational level the validity of criticisms directed against them is acknowledged. An example should make this point clearer.

One of the college of education lecturers interviewed by Macaulay in Glasgow drew a distinction between a Glasgow accent, to which he said he had no objection, and 'careless speech where they're clipping word endings and drawing out vowels' (Macaulay, 1977:109). The features characterising 'careless speech' quoted by the lecturer appear, in fact, to be two important components of the Glasgow accent – the length of certain vowels relative to their southern Standard British English equivalents and the glottal stop. Although, to be sure there is variation in the capacity of individuals to exploit the resources of the language (see Fillmore, 1979 for a stimulating discussion of variation in individual language ability), features of an arbitrary and socially distributed kind such as we have been discussing are not relevant to that variation. It is simply not possible to distinguish reliably between 'a local accent' (which, of course, ranges along the careful to casual continuum) and 'careless speech'. To do so is to demonstrate the pervasive influence of prescriptive ideologies, even while seeming to reject them. In view of the pressures on the Glasgow lecturer to inculcate norms of correctness in his students, it seems reasonably clear that open discussion and rigorous analysis would help him (and others who face similar problems) to clarify the issues involved. At the moment, educationalists are often subject to demands that they should teach pupils to speak and write English 'properly', without any clear indication of how this should be done, or appreciation of what is implied in the task.

In view, then, of this general and pervasive difficulty associated with an open discussion of prescriptivism, it might be helpful to move into a less familiar social context and examine the character and consequences of prescriptivism there. One very interesting geographical area for examining this topic, where it has been well documented, is Singapore.

Singapore, a former British colony, is a prosperous multilingual and multi-ethnic community with four official languages: these are Tamil, English, Malay and Chinese. Government policy has deliberately encouraged linguistic and cultural pluralism for many reasons, not least of which is the desire to avoid inter-ethnic conflict (Platt and Weber, 1980:129). It is Singapore English, rather than the other official languages, which concerns us here.

English has spread rapidly, even since independence, either as a first language or as a medium of education for non-native speakers (Platt and Weber, 1980). The actual range of varieties of English is much greater than is found in the British Isles. On the one hand we can speak of an *acrolect* or high status variety, and on the other a *basilect* or low status variety, with the *mesolect* occupying the intermediate position. These terms are usually descriptive of what is known as a *post-creole continuum* – that is the range of non-discrete varieties in a post-colonial situation ranging from the acrolect, which is generally very close to the standard language of the colonial power, through to the basilect, which structurally resembles a creole. It is sufficient here to characterise a creole as a mixed language, resulting historically from contact between speakers of different and mutually unintelligible languages. Creoles are usually associated with colonial situations and are generally assigned a very low social status. Basilectal speakers, who occupy the lowest position in a post-creole continuum, are often quite unintelligible to speakers of the acrolect. All speakers occupy a range on this acrolect-basilect continuum, which correlates closely with their social status, shifting along it according to social context in much the same way as British speakers manipulate linguistic variables. Of course, the extent of linguistic difference is much greater. Such continua have been described in Jamaica by de Camp (1971) and in Guyana by Bickerton (1975), and it is likely, we should note, that these studies will be of increasing relevance to an understanding of the sociolinguistic structure of ethnic minority communities in Britain. A detailed account of the structure and function of pidgins and creoles is not directly relevant here, but interested readers are referred to Todd (1974) for a lucid introductory account of the social, political and linguistic issues involved.

In Singapore, a very distinctive *non-British* acrolectal variety of English is gradually emerging, to the extent that it is now possible to speak of Singaporean English as a variety of English in its own right. Similar comments could be made, of course, about a great many post-colonial speech communities. Examples of Singaporean features, observed in the speech of radio announcers, university staff and business executives, include different stress and intonation patterns from those of RP, and deletion of final /d/ and /t/ in consonant clusters in words like *conflict, invest, end* and *hold*. One phrase quoted by Platt (1977) is 'the res*t* of Southeas*t* Asia'. Standard accents of British English do not commonly delete final /t/ in this manner before vowels, although, as we have seen, it is usually deleted between consonants.

One syntactic feature which is very characteristic of Singaporean English and appears to be gaining currency, even in written varieties, is the expression *use to* as a mark of habitual aspect. Thus, *all Europeans use to go there* is glossed as 'Europeans commonly go there'.

A great many distinctive characteristics like this can be listed which, according to empirical evidence, appear regularly in the speech of even a highly educated Singaporean. Although some of them are certainly found more frequently in informal discourse than in more formal discussions, it seems inappropriate to label them 'substandard' as does, for example, Tongue (1974). The point is that they are there; and as their use appears to be increasing in educated speech, simply to treat them as inferior evades the important question of how the emergence of this variety should affect educational policy. Should, for example, syntactic features like *use to* be acknowledged as existing, and incorporated into grammars of Singaporean English? Should Singaporean children be taught that syntactic features are wrong because they do not coincide with British norms? Should Singaporean students taking public examinations which are administered and assessed in Britain be penalised for using features which are regularly distributed among educated Singaporeans? At present, the position is that they are being so penalised, and although it may be possible to argue that such a policy is appropriate, at least examiners should be aware of the linguistic facts and the matter opened to debate. For as Platt and Weber point out, 'there is a limit to the effect of even the most skilfully contrived language programme if it is too much out of step with the speech patterns within a community' (p. 196). Moreover, there is evidence that influential Singaporeans, such as businessmen and politicians, wish (as we might expect) to identify themselves, when they speak, as Singaporeans rather than Englishmen.

It seems fairly clear that in this dynamic developing situation, prescription of a set of norms which are not used and not heard simply will not work, and is unlikely to be an adequate basis for a sound language teaching programme. One writer demonstrates this by describing the tongue-tying effect of inappropriate prescription on Chinese-medium educated students in Singapore who learn English as a second language:

> The English you learn in school is not in fact the English most commonly used in Singapore, and your teacher is spending a lot of time trying to break you of habits which you know to be perfectly acceptable in Singapore. In fact, by following your teacher's rules, you suspect that you may find yourself less able to communicate easily, for you feel you'll be so conscious of 'rules' that you'll be tongue-tied. (Lynn, 1972:115 – quoted in Platt and Weber)

This discussion of Singapore English has been introduced for two main reasons. First, it demonstrates that prescriptive attitudes are quite widespread, and that they tend to be rather similar wherever they are found. In their most illiberal form, they are characterised by a resistance to (or ignorance of) the facts of language use, and by the tendency noted by Platt and Weber to view as inferior even well-established usage which does not conform to a largely irrelevant idealised norm. The new norm in Singapore is, of course, associated with socio-economic changes after the departure of the colonial power.

Second, the educationally damaging and generally inadequate character of the prescriptions is revealed rather clearly when attempts are made to enforce them in a multilingual community like Singapore where the range of variation is so much greater than in Britain and where successful English teaching is explicitly acknowledged to be a matter of social and political importance. It is easier to demonstrate from Singaporean data than from British that over-prescriptivism forms an inadequate approach to reconciling the need for good standard language teaching with due recognition of speakers' existing language patterns. However, the substance of most critical comment is very similar in both places.

This point is made implicitly by Platt and Weber when they point out the relevance of Trudgill's book, *Accent, Dialect and the School* for Singaporean educators. This book, designed for British teachers, does not set out to analyse the social and political forces underlying prescriptivism; but it is valuable as a clear and relatively untechnical account of the range of variation in the British speech community and the social meaning of that variation. As well as containing a critique of prescriptive attitudes, the book lays out a range of strategic options open to teachers who need to teach a control of Standard English to non-standard speakers. Platt and Weber strongly endorse the central argument that any attempt to eliminate or stigmatise a non-standard variety will not work, and will be seen as a direct attack on the values and social identity of the speaker. They strongly favour the alternative approach of teaching the child, quite explicitly, facts about the way in which different social and regional varieties are related to each other, so bringing him to an understanding of the social functions and structural characteristics of the standard language.

These comments by Platt and Weber on prescriptivism in Singapore are extremely illuminating. However, many more instances could be quoted of the damaging effects of prescriptive ideologies in post-colonial multilingual societies where the question of which language to choose as the medium of broadcasting, education and public communication is an important social and political issue. One of the most interesting cases is the emergence of the creole, New Guinea Pidgin, as the national language of Papua New Guinea – an area described as a 'sociolinguistic laboratory' (Wurm, ed., 1979).

For various reasons, New Guinea Pidgin rather than English fulfils this role best, and has, in fact, developed functionally and structurally to the point of being adequate for the purpose. At present, the situation in Papua New Guinea is as follows:

> In the eyes of the great majority of the indigenous population of Papua New Guinea, the status of NGP has increased immeasurably since self-government and independence, and the language has become elevated into social functions formerly reserved for English. It is now the almost exclusive debate language of the Papua New Guinea parliament; it is now possible

for it to be resorted to in education, its use is now permitted and is very much in evidence on premises from which it was formerly barred, such as the University of Papua New Guinea (Wurm and Mühlhäusler, 1979:247)

The general consensus of expert opinion, as reported by Mühlhäusler (1979:577), is that New Guinea Pidgin will soon officially have the status of a national language, while English will remain the official language for higher education and for the nation's dealings with the outside world. Education appears to be the domain in which the use of pidgin is at present increasing, at the expense of English. However, scholars who have been concerned with the linguistic technicalities of standardisation (such as developing an orthography, a dictionary and a grammar) report extremely negative attitudes to New Guinea Pidgin, usually on the part of ex-colonial expatriates (see Mühlhäusler, 1979). These attitudes, in which New Guinea Pidgin is viewed as 'not a proper language', are inaccurate, needlessly insulting to the large number of native speakers for whom it has a high prestige (see Sankoff, 1972 for an earlier account of this) and insensitive to the need of a recently independent multilingual state to develop a common language which is acceptable to the largest possible number of its speakers.

5.5 Group identity and language variation

The remainder of this chapter explores one particular issue which has already emerged briefly several times.

In their discussion of prescriptivism in Scotland (see p. 100 above), Romaine and Reid point out the importance of distinguishing two types of sociolinguistic norm. First, there is what they describe as the *social norm*. This is the kind of norm of which speakers are explicitly aware and which refers to the wider social acceptability of linguistic variants. Speakers show their sensitivity to this norm by moving towards it in careful styles where they use (for example) the glottal stop with diminishing frequency. But the fact that the glottal stop is actually used overall a good deal by Glasgow speakers (74 per cent of all possible occasions of use) suggests that this linguistic element constitutes another kind of norm which runs quite counter to the social norm. This might be called the community norm. (The distinction between *community norm* and *social norm* is anticipated to some extent in our discussion in Chapter 3 on overt and formal, as against covert and informal, mechanisms of language maintenance.) The same tension between the two types of norm is reflected in the opposition between the zero form of /h/ and the presence of [h]; the *-in'* form and the *-ing* form of the present continuous verb inflection (see p. 92 above). Also, it was hinted at in our account of Singapore English: Singaporeans certainly view standard British English as in a sense superior and the 'ideal' form of English; but at the same time they want to sound like Singaporeans, not like Englishmen.

We have already seen that the hierarchical structure of modern Western society is closely mirrored (and reinforced) by these patterns of relatively low level linguistic differentiation. In all cities, there are linguistic hierarchies which correspond to social hierarchies, and the persons of highest status with greatest potential for exercising power are always speakers of the linguistic variety which is judged to be the most logical, beautiful and comprehensible.

Consequently, the social and political pressure on persons in cities to give up speaking their own dialects, which are regarded as inferior, is considerable. The same may be said of the pressure on ethno-linguistic groups with a strong sense of their own distinctiveness, like speakers of Black English in the United States, Canadian French in Canada, Jamaican Creole in Britain or Lowland Scots in Southern Scotland. As a consequence, we find in developed countries like Britain a curious paradox. On the one hand we have linguistic stratification acting as a reflection of social stratification with persons indicating their eagerness to adopt higher status speech norms by style-shifting towards them in asymmetrical social situations; this much the urban language surveys have clearly shown. On the other hand we have evidence of very great stability, often over centuries, of socially disfavoured varieties. Why should this be? Why should speakers continue to use language in accordance with the community norm when it seems clear that the benefits of adopting the social norm would be very much greater? (see also the discussion of informal language maintenance, Chapter 3.2) An answer to this question is plainly relevant to those involved in teaching language with reference to the social norm, and may, in fact, have a bearing on educational strategy.

It has emerged from a number of studies that speakers of socially disfavoured dialects or languages often acquiesce to the unfavourable judgments made by society at large about the way they speak;

but this is far from the whole story. These same low-status languages and dialects are frequently seen as an important symbol of group cohesion and identity (see Ryan, 1979 for a discussion of this issue). In addition to such work on attitudes to language, a number of quantitative sociolinguistic studies have looked at the link between an individual's relationship to others in a small-scale social group, and the extent to which he uses a socially disfavoured language variety. Generally, these studies take as their units pre-existing social groups rather than, like the large scale surveys such as those in Glasgow, Bradford and Norwich, individuals representative of the larger community who may then be grouped according to their social class characteristics. As it turns out, the community norm is best investigated by focusing on pre-existing groups.

Two of the best known of these studies are by William Labov, the first of the language of Martha's Vineyard, an island off the coast of Massachusetts, and the second of the language of adolescent gang members, in Harlem, New York City. In Martha's Vineyard, Labov focused on the realisations of the diphthongs /ay/ and /aw/ (as in *mice* and *mouse*). He interviewed a number of speakers drawn from different ages and ethnic groups on the island, and noted that among the younger speakers a movement seemed to be taking place *away from* the pronunciations associated with the standard New England social norm, and *towards* a pronunciation associated with conservative and characteristically Vineyard speakers. The heaviest users of this type of pronunciation were young men who actively sought to identify themselves as Vineyarders, rejected the values of the mainland, and resented the encroachment of wealthy summer visitors on the traditional island way of life. Thus, these speakers seem to be exploiting the resources of the non-standard dialect as a way of projecting their social identities in much the same way as the Singaporeans who do not want to sound like Englishmen. Also as in Singapore, this pattern emerges despite extensive exposure of speakers to the educational system; some college educated boys in Martha's Vineyard were extremely heavy users of the vernacular vowels.

The second of Labov's studies which concerns us here focused on American Black English Vernacular – a variety of English widely considered to be of very inferior status. One aspect of the investigation revealed a connection between a speaker's language and his place in a peer group network structure; three informally constituted peer groups were studied, known as the Jets, Cobras and Thunderbirds.

Variable deletion of the copula (the verb *to be*) is a feature of Black English Vernacular which Labov studied quantitatively in the manner described earlier in this chapter. In a sequence like *He is a bad man* the copula could either appear or be replaced by *He a bad man*. The zero form is an important community norm of BEV. Effectively, Labov was able to relate incidence of copula deletion to the extent to which speakers were integrated into Black English vernacular culture. To do this, he concentrated particularly on the group known as the Jets, and it is worth reporting his findings in a little detail.

There were two centres for the Jets based on the two apartment blocks where they lived: a core group was associated with each centre. Depending on each member's habitual associates and on who (reciprocally) regarded whom as a friend, Labov was able to specify four degrees of integration into the vernacular culture which, in turn, he viewed as dependent on peer group structure. At one extreme are the core members who are at the centre, then secondary members, peripheral members and finally *lames*. The lames are isolated individuals, effectively outside the street culture. Their use of the zero form of the copula (20 per cent) is very much less than that of the core and secondary members who use it 46 per cent of the time and rather less than the peripheral members who score 26 per cent. Thus, a speaker's place in a group structure can be seen to be reflected quite closely by his language. Labov is at pains to emphasise that it is the normal, active, healthy youth who is the strongest user of the vernacular, while the relatively standardised speakers (the lames) are, for one reason or another, social isolates on the edge of a group to which they would like to claim membership.

It has now become apparent that the function of non-standard language as a marker of group identity revealed by these studies is in no sense a socially marginal phenomenon, but is deeply rooted in the language behaviour of communities everywhere. Bearing this point in mind, it is worth noting Labov's more recent comments (1980:263) on the subject of American Black English. He points out that the division between black and white speech in the United States is increasing, and that this schism is clearly associated with a renewed sense of black pride, a strenuous reassertion of local rights and privileges by black groups who hold them, and a demand for a fair share of jobs and opportunities. Labov also remarks that if we want to understand how language is used in cities, we must take account of *both* the kinds of 'prestige' which seem to attach themselves to language – the status-oriented and the identity-oriented. This corresponds to the distinction which we have made here between social norms and community norms, which, in terms of their influence on language use, appear to pull in opposite directions. If we consider the implications of Labov's findings in Harlem and in Martha's Vineyard, we begin to understand why so many speakers in cities continue to use stigmatised linguistic features; the projection of group identity appears, for some speakers, to be more important than the acceptance of the social norm with its associated meanings of power and status.

These observations may be related to patterns of language use among black speakers in Britain, although we must bear in mind that research into the language usage patterns of non-indigenous communities here is still in its infancy. Nevertheless, interesting pioneer work on the problems faced by the creole-speaking child of West Indian origin has been carried out by a number of scholars many of whom are (or have been) practising teachers. The contributions of V.K. Edwards, Sutcliffe and Hewitt are quite explicitly a response to the problems encountered by these children and their teachers.

Both Hewitt and Edwards suggest that the use of creole is actually *increasing*, and, like Labov, relate this increase to the function of creole as a powerful symbol of community identity. The fluency of creole speakers in spoken and written Standard English appears to vary immensely, and conversely some children are more fluent in creole (described as *patois* by the West Indian community) than others.

A number of educators have commented on the use made by children of creole as a means of expressing group solidarity and identity; yet it is frequently described as low status or inferior, both by members of the white community and by its users. However, like the non-standard dialects we have been considering, its use apparently constitutes a powerful community norm, to the extent that (according to the Select Committee on Race Relations and Immigration) many West Indian children actually *begin* using creole in their early teens. Up until that point, they have apparently used the local dialect (Hewitt, 1982). (The apparently sudden appearance of creole in adolescence may well reflect no more the absence of systematic studies of its use among young children; adolescent creole speakers have most probably used creole in less visible social contexts since early childhood. If this is so, it is the context of use that changes, not the repertoire available to speakers. Interestingly, it appears that the prestige which creole enjoys at community level attracts children from other ethnic groups. According to Hewitt, 'cases of Turkish and Greek children using creole forms are not uncommon... However, the most notable trend has been the acquisition of creole by white British working class children as an additional linguistic skill' (1982:222). Thus it would appear that, if we are to understand the educational problems of Jamaican children, we must take account of creole as a powerful symbol of identity in the black community, rather than simply accepting the 'inferior' label. This is not to deny the importance of teaching skill in Standard English.

As we suggested in the previous section, what is involved is the incorporation into teaching strategy of a positive recognition that a child's linguistic competence may be very much greater than is suggested by his ability in Standard English. Certainly, we cannot assume that West Indian children will simply stop using creole, and attempts within the educational system to ignore it are likely to have socially undesirable consequences. As Edwards points out, over-prescriptivism in relation to creole gives rise to neglect and inappropriate teaching strategies, such as those quoted by Townsend and Brittan:

> As the West Indians officially speak English no special allowance of staff is given.
>
> Boys of West Indian origin: In each year we have a class for retarded pupils. Although not designed as such, all of these classes have about 90 per cent West Indians or pupils of West Indian origin. (Townsend and Brittan, 1972:76)

The most obvious argument against the prescriptivism implied in these policies (i.e. insisting that creole speakers are no different from indigenous English speakers) is simply that it will not have the desired effect. Very largely for the various social and attitudinal reasons discussed in this chapter, it is an ineffective way of tackling the language problems of West Indian children. Moreover, given the state of race relations in Britain at the time of writing (1984), any attempt to teach Standard English without sympathetic appreciation of the status of creole would, in the words of Edwards, 'inevitably be interpreted as yet another act of oppression in a climate where patois usage is a symbol of black identity' (V.K. Edwards, 1981:7). Happily, the attitudes of earlier years have now been mòdified a little and the language needs of West Indians are being discussed more openly as the significance of the socio-linguistic facts is beginning to be appreciated. We shall have more to say in the following chapter about the social circumstances in which creole is used, and in which switching between creole and English takes place.

Meantime, readers are referred to the discussion of language *maintenance* in Chapter 3 (see p. 57 above), where it was suggested that the characteristic network structures of poor communities con-stituted important mechanisms for the maintenance of low-status linguistic codes. The concept of social network as discussed there (and see also Milroy, 1980) helps us to understand the capacity of stigmatised varieties like Jamaican creole in Britain to survive in the face of strong counter-pressures.

5.6   Conclusion

We have tried to show in this chapter that social structure, at various levels, is closely connected with language variability of the kind which is usually the subject of prescriptive comment. Moreover, the tendency of low status language varieties to persist, and even to become more widespread in certain social conditions, is in no sense a marginal phenomenon which those concerned with language teaching and assessment can afford to dismiss. This capacity for long term survival which stigmatised language varieties demonstrate is quite contrary to the popular view that modern mass education and mass communication will have a standardising effect on language; in fact, there are even signs that as a result of increased pressure from low status groups, non-standard varieties are to a certain extent becoming publicly legitimised. It seems appropriate to conclude this chapter with an account of a well-known legal judgment which exemplifies not only this recent trend, but the social importance of developing means of dealing with the educa-tional problems of non-standard speakers.

The so-called 'Black English Trial' took place in Ann Arbor, Michigan, during the summer of 1979. The plaintiffs – parents of some black children who were progressing extremely badly at school – argued that the authorities had failed to take account of cultural, social and economic factors which would prevent the children from making normal progress. In fact, the case was ultimately argued on whether the authorities had taken action to overcome *linguistic* barriers which might impede the children's progress.

The plaintiffs presented linguistic evidence of a very detailed kind, and the judge's ruling was that the authorities' failure to recognize Black English as a separate language system meant that the children were handicapped in learning to read and write Standard English. Thus, in effect, unless their language problems were treated seriously, their social mobility was blocked. The authorities were ordered to take specific steps to remedy the situation. We do not wish to pursue here the technical question of whether Black English generally (including British Black English) should be regarded as a linguistic system separate from the standard. What seems to be required in both Britain and the United States is that the quite extensive differences between Black English and Standard English should be taken into account by education authorities in a non-evaluative way.

Clearly, a judgment of this kind has profound implications, which educators and others concerned with language teaching and assessment are still attempting to explore. (See Whiteman, 1980 for a number of early reactions and Labov, 1982 for an extremely lucid account of the case.) For example, one of the specific complaints at the trial was that assessment methods (in this case the Wepman Auditory Discrimination Test) did not take account of the structural characteristics of the children's phonological systems. Consequently they were assessed as being deaf, or as having perceptual disorders and placed in remedial classes, when in fact they were perfectly normal.

We shall see shortly that this is not the only documented example of linguistically inadequate assessment techniques, interpreted by linguistically naive assessors, being used to support notions of the inadequacy of non-standard dialects and their speakers.

It is important to note the emphasis placed by the judge, the plaintiffs and the expert witnesses on the need for effective teaching of Standard English. The educational purpose of understanding the structure of Black English or any other non-standard code is to fulfil that aim; not, as is often argued, to abandon any attempt to teach Standard English. A more general point is that a modern democratic educational system needs to develop means of making the standard form of the language available as a resource to all pupils.

This involves a careful scrutiny of the role of prescriptive ideologies in educational theory and practice, and in language assessment. We have hardly begun such a scrutiny in this country. What is clear is that dissemination of the standard and its use as a medium of education cannot be accomplished by stigmatising and ignoring non-standard varieties. Their patterns of use are too closely associated with what appear to be very general patterns both of small-scale community structure and of larger-scale social structure to allow such an easy solution.

We move on now to consider in a little more detail the range of language used by speakers in different social situations. The following chapters will examine the implications of work in this area for the education and assessment of non-standard speakers.

6

Linguistic repertoires and communicative competence

6.1 Introductory

In Chapters 4 and 5 we related questions of correctness to variation in language use according to social factors such as region, class and sex of speaker. Now we look more closely at variation according to *occasion of use*.

Peter Trudgill has made a useful distinction between two different types of 'mistake' which are the subject of prescriptive comment. The first involves linguistic elements which have a regular distribution; the second concerns 'features which are quite natural to all native speakers, and are a part of standard English, as well as other dialects, but which many people still feel rather uncomfortable about' (1975:42). Thus compare the following alternatives:

it's me : it is I
it was him that did it : it was he who did it.

The first sentence in each pair would often be said to be a 'mistake', although most standard speakers (whether they are conscious of it or not) would almost certainly choose those sentence types rather than their alternatives when they are speaking informally, and would feel that such a choice was more 'natural'. Thus some notions of what is 'correct' seem to be associated not with the social distribution of linguistic variants, but with their distribution according to occasion of use; the choice appropriate to the more formal occasion is usually said to be the 'correct' form of the language. It is this second notion of correctness with which we are concerned here. We may note, first of all, that in some way a respect for high standards of literacy is involved; the second sentence in each pair is distinctly 'bookish'. Furthermore, there seems to be an assumption that written English 'sets the standard' for a uniquely correct form of spoken English.

Both of these attitudes to correctness have emerged during discussion in earlier chapters. In this chapter and the next, we look systematically at their implications.

6.2 Communicative competence

It is, in fact, quite clear that all speakers vary their language very extensively according to situation; there are, as Labov has pointed out, no single-style speakers. The capacity of persons to select and recognise the language variety appropriate to the occasion is known as their *communicative competence*. Since it is often this aspect of language choice which underlies prescriptive comment, an exploration of exactly what constitutes communicative competence is relevant here.

As this discussion will necessarily range over an extensive area, it will be helpful to note, prospectively, that it is introduced for three reasons. We discuss communicative competence not only as a part of our commentary on notions of correctness, but as a means of elucidating what a speaker's *language ability* might consist of. For prescriptive comment is frequently expressed as an apparently valid argument that a speaker's language is in some sense 'poor' or 'deficient'. Clearly, in order to assess the validity of an argument of this kind, we need to have some idea of what 'normal' language ability might consist of. Finally, when we examine language proficiency tests, which are designed to measure language ability, it will be clear that an understanding of what is involved in communicative competence helps us assess their rigour and validity.

The notion of communicative competence was introduced by Dell Hymes, who considered such a theoretical construct to be important in characterising the way language was actually used in a community, as opposed to the way it might be constructed *by an ideal speaker-hearer* of the kind postulated by Chomsky:

> No normal person and no normal community is limited in repertoire to a single variety or code, to an unchanging monotony which would preclude the possibility of indicating respect, insolence, mock seriousness, role distance, etc., by switching from one variety to another. (1967:9)

Hymes's basic unit of analysis is the *speech event*. This may be quite an extensive stretch of discourse, but is analytically parallel to the *sentence* as a basic syntactic unit. Speech events are frequently recognised in communities as entities sufficiently clear to merit a label, such as (for example) *prayer, joke, interview, harangue*. Hymes argues that a speaker's ability to recognise and use the language appropriate to a given speech event may be viewed as an aspect of his communicative competence. The totality of styles (both spoken and written) available to a community is known as its *linguistic repertoire*, and speakers learn to select from this repertoire in order to fill various communicative needs, such as those outlined by Hymes. Thus part of the communicative competence of a British school-teacher might be a command of the styles needed for the following purposes: addressing a formal meeting; teaching a class; writing a formal report; writing an informal letter; addressing his baby son; telling a joke; and chatting to his friends in a pub over a beer.

The formal linguistic characteristics of all these styles are, as most of us are intuitively aware, likely to be quite divergent, although little progress has been made in studying them. The reasons for this slow progress are considered shortly. We may also note at this stage that the capacity of the teacher to control the styles appropriately to formal, public discourse (such as addressing meetings, teaching classes and writing reports) is likely to be crucial in his general career and economic advancement, although these styles reflect only a fraction of his communicative competence. Thus, just as class and regional accents are not viewed as being all of equal value so speech events are not viewed as being all of equal value. The basis of the evaluative measures is again not purely linguistic but is associated with what is publicly functional in the larger society outside family and personal network. Clearly, such an evaluation is a practical one, and reflects a social reality; for such public styles tend, in Gillian Brown's terms, to be *message-oriented* rather than *listener-oriented*. By this, she means that they tend to be directed towards a specific goal, the whole point of a message-oriented utterance being the 'communication of a propositional or cognitive (information bearing) message to the listener' (Brown, 1982:77).

Listener-oriented utterances, on the other hand, tend to be associated with an informal range of styles of the kind exemplified in the last paragraph but one. When a man talking to his baby son, or chatting to his friends in the pub, he is likely to be concerned principally with establishing or maintaining a relationship with the listener; the exact information content of the message is less important. This distinction between message-oriented and listener-oriented seems to us to be a useful one although, as Brown points out, many utterances in practice contain elements of both types.

When a child is unable to handle public styles (which generally involves an inability to produce message-oriented utterances appropriately), this inability is often criticised as an inability to handle language *generally*. But incompetence in public styles should not be equated with general linguistic inadequacy (which is often implicitly associated with lack of cognitive ability). What is clear is that children who can chat away quite happily to their friends, but who cannot handle message-oriented utterances, need instruction *quite specifically* in that area of their repertoires. Gillian Brown has already made a useful and practical beginning here by enumerating the most prominent formal characteristics of message-oriented utterances and suggesting the outlines of a teaching programme.

We need to make a further point about the rather different communicative competences controlled by different speakers. For a number of reasons which are not always entirely obvious, but are related to various social, cultural and economic factors (discussed by, for example, Gumperz, 1982:77), relatively educated and high status speakers are likely to have the firmest command of public and formal styles. It does not follow at all from this (as is sometimes assumed) that low status speakers command little or no stylistic variety in their linguistic repertoires; the point is that they are likely to be competent in a different range of styles. This competence is of relevance to any assessment of the educational potential of a child; for while it is clear that an important job of a public education system is to teach control of *formal* styles, in practice the task is often not consistently defined in this way. As we have noted, inadequacies in this part of the repertoire are often viewed as *general* linguistic inadequacies. Alternatively, as both Brown (1982) and Gannon (1982) note, a more liberal approach is sometimes adopted of not distinguishing between one part of the repertoire and another, but encouraging children to express themselves in the manner most natural and congenial to them. Clearly if there is a *specific* stylistic problem, this strategy will be of little value. What does appear to be needed is a systematic account of various types of linguistic repertoire; for the linguistic repertoire is the raw material from which a speaker builds his communicative competence.

6.3 Types of linguistic repertoire

It is important to note that a linguistic repertoire may cut across more than one language, with switching from one language to another, or to a mixture, taking place in much the same circumstances as style switching in monolingual repertoire. It is for this reason that studies of bilingual code-switching are of relevance to the understanding of monolingual style shifting. Bilingual code-switching has, in fact, been more extensively studied, probably because the switching process is particularly visible. One interesting example of such a study dates from the 1960s, when it was reported that 92% of the population of Paraguay were bilingual in Guarani and Spanish, with both languages having official status. There was little sign that this bilingualism was a temporary phenomenon which would disappear as the population became monolingual in Spanish. Factors such as whether conversation was taking place in an urban or rural setting, the intimacy of the relationship between the interlocutors and the topic of conversation, all influenced language choice in much the same way as they influence stylistic choice in English (see Trudgill, 1983 for a discussion of the Paraguayan linguistic repertoire).

A great many interesting studies have been carried out of the circumstances in which speakers move between different elements in their repertoires. For example, Denison (1972) reported his observations made in 1960 in the village of Sauris, in the Italian Alps, of how speakers moved between Italian, Friulian, and German. The main factors which determined language choice concerned the setting of the interaction (German was usually confined to domestic contexts), the participants, and the topic. Friulian was usually used in interactions with other locals outside the home, and Denison showed how persons could manipulate their repertoires for social and personal reasons. He described, for example, how one woman, who was trying to compel her husband to leave the bar where he was drinking, used German, the language of domesticity, in a context where Friulian would be the normal choice. Thus she selected German consciously or unconsciously, for clearly manipulative purposes. (The situation now in Sauris is that German is no longer used: the repertoire consists of Friulian and Italian.)

In a study of the linguistic repertoire of Hemnesberget, a small town in Northern Norway, Blom and Gumperz (1972) have documented in detail the manner in which speakers use standard Norwegian and Norwegian dialect, both recognisable elements in the repertoire. Again, the principles underlying dialect switching seem to be similar to those which underlie style shifting and language switching. One group of speakers, aptly described as members of the 'local team', use the dialect at all times with other locals, and are restricted in their use of the standard to contexts where it conveys 'meanings of officiality, expertise and politeness to strangers who are clearly segmented from their personal life' (1972:434). In complete contrast, the élite of the town view the standard as their norm, and use the dialect only for a special effect of some kind such as in telling jokes or adding local colour to an anecdote. Overuse of the standard is viewed by locals as an unfriendly act of dissociation, and as a sign of contempt for local values, while the élite on the other hand seems to view the dialect as symbolising low status and lack of education.

This study, along with many others, shows the socially functional nature of a varied repertoire. For example, Blom and Gumperz view the perceived dichotomy between the standard and dialect, and the maintenance of both codes, as functional, in that their manipulation allows important social meanings to be expressed. They are maintained by a social system which sharply distinguishes between local and non-local norms and values. It is this important social function of variation which seems to explain why communities maintain distinctive codes, even when one of the codes is publicly considered to be of low status. For in Norway or Sauris or Paraguay it would seem from a commonsense point of view to be simpler to use a single code. However, although governments may often go to considerable lengths to persuade or even compel communities to adopt monolingual repertoires (as, for example, in Wales until quite recently), communities do not always seem to view the adoption of a monolingual repertoire as useful or functional, and it is easy to see how the resources of a fairly clearly differentiated repertoire can be manipulated for a range of social and affective purposes and so be viewed as extremely functional.

Some recent work on West Indian immigrant children in London (see also p. 112 above) shows how this works in practice. It appears that speakers, far from abandoning low status portions of the repertoire, are actually extending, for social purposes, the use of creole. Creole is not, as might be expected, disappearing from the repertoire of children born and educated in this country who now have a perfect command of English. As we have seen, not only do *black* adolescents use creole increasingly as they emerge from childhood to adolescence, but *white* adolescents also use creole with black friends. However, white use of creole is restricted to interactions with extremely close friends, and it is reported that where a white speaker with black friends is joined by more black friends unknown to the white speaker, the rule is that the white speaker must refrain from using creole until a context of friendliness and trust has developed. If he attempts to use creole simply to signal friendliness, he risks provoking hostility. Thus, knowledge of when and when not to use creole in this socially volatile context is a delicate matter requiring some judgment and sensitivity (Hewitt, 1982).

One other study of a linguistic repertoire is of particular interest to us here. Beatriz Lavandera (1978) has studied the language of Italian immigrants to Buenos Aires, Argentina, who have developed a special form of Spanish known as *cocoliche*. This variety of Spanish is of extremely low status and is a frequent butt of stage humour, rather like Irish English in Britain.

Lavandera's study is of interest mainly because it examines in some detail the structural characteristics of the Italian community's total repertoire and assesses the validity or otherwise of the attitudes of the Spanish-speaking majority to *cocoliche*. It emerges that while *cocoliche* is popularly characterised as a reduced and defective form of Spanish, it is, in fact, rich in inflexions and other linguistic devices for conveying referential meaning and so not at all impoverished in terms of its core linguistic components. However, what *cocoliche* appears specifically to lack is that stylistic variation inherent in Argentine Spanish which performs a crucial function in fulfilling the total communicative needs of the speech community. To demonstrate this, Lavandera identifies, amongst other elements, the variable (s) in Argentine Spanish which is realised as three variants, [s], [h] and zero in word final and preconsonantal positions (cf. the discussion of the sociolinguistic variable on p. 92 above). *Cocoliche* speakers appear almost invariably to use the zero variant in word final positions and the [s] variant in preconsonantal positions.

Thus, while monolingual Spanish-speaking Argentines would variably use [s] and zero to realise the final segment of a word like *nos*, 'us', Italian Argentines almost categorically use the zero variant. Similarly, while /s/ in preconsonantal positions in words like *esperar*, 'hope', is variably realised by monolinguals as [h] and [s], Italian Argentines categorically use the [s] variant in this phonetic context. Since forms with [s] are of higher prestige in *both* environments, it is not the case that the immigrants are simply selecting the less prestigious variant. Rather, it seems to be an unconstrained distribution of a socially and stylistically variable element which principally connotes the 'foreignness' of the accent, and, as Lavandera (1978:391) points out, *cocoliche* speakers are unable to 'exploit a signal which is systematically used by native speakers to distinguish styles and consequently to characterize speech events'. The point is that this categorical treatment of what is for native speakers a variable element (in much the same way as (ng) is a variable element in English) seems to be perceived by monolingual Argentines as a simplification of the structure of Spanish and evidence of a defective control of the language. It is important to remember, however, that this lack of stylistic differentiation within Spanish does not seem to hinder the expression of *referential* meaning. The fact that the linguistic capacity of Italian Argentines should nevertheless be judged negatively by native speakers in this way is evidence of the important communicative function of variable linguistic elements such as (s).

It is worth stressing that although *cocoliche* speakers cannot exploit the variable resources of Spanish in such a way as to express, for example, solidarity or social distance, they do control other mechanisms for conveying these social meanings; they switch between *cocoliche* and Italian dialect. Thus, if the linguistic ability of bilingual speakers is assessed with reference to *only* one of their languages, rather than with reference to the total repertoire, it is likely that they will be judged as inadequate; this is not surprising, as they are being given the opportunity to display only a small part of their communicative competence. We have already noted a parallel tendency for low status monolingual speakers of English to be judged as linguistically inadequate, again on the evidence of a similarly small part of the repertoire.

The important conclusion which we may draw here from Lavandera's work is that judgments about the adequacy or otherwise of a speaker's language may hinge in a complicated way on the existence in a community of varied repertoires and varied communicative competences. The issue of whether a speaker can adequately convey referential meaning seems to be irrelevant to the formulation of such judgments; but the low status of the speakers is, of course, highly relevant. However, those judgments about language ability which are implicit judgments of communicative competence should, if they are to be equitable, be based on a much wider notion of 'language ability' than is customary. All the linguistic research which has been carried out into the nature of communicative competence suggests that this conclusion is relevant also to the language behaviour of *monolingual* speakers. With this comment in mind, we turn now to a brief consideration of formal measures of language ability.

6.4 Some practical considerations

It is a fault of *language proficiency* measures generally, and one for which they have received a great deal of criticism, that they do not measure language use in specific situations. Rather, they collect their data by means of standardised, well-controlled experimental types of procedure which differ considerably from everyday communicative events. Such a procedure is compared by Klein and Dittmar (1979:87) to that of testing swimming by having a group of people swim three lengths in a pool of water one foot deep. This test method would certainly not ensure that the best swimmer finished first (although this might happen by chance) and quite different skills would unintentionally be tested.

Klein and Dittmar are making here a point very similar to ours: that language assessment of all kinds, whether of native speakers, immigrants or foreign language learners is of dubious validity as a measure of language ability unless it takes account of the facts of communicative competence. Such competence is by its nature variable and sensitive to situation, and so a test situation cannot hope to make a fair assessment of linguistic ability. Moreover, as we shall see, the *kind* of language recognised as appropriate in assessments may bear little relation to the kind of language used in non-test situations. Thus, a speaker may be judged as linguistically competent or incompetent on a very narrow and inadequate linguistic basis, and we shall be arguing in Chapter 8 that unacknowledged prescriptive norms underlie many supposedly objective numerical scores derived from language tests.

It is quite clear, however, that a great many people professionally concerned with language know very well that the language observed to be used by speakers in an asymmetrical social situation is likely to represent only a tiny fraction of their linguistic repertoire. A recent study of the prescriptive linguistic attitudes of teacher-training college lecturers has shown that even persons who are prepared to make very harsh prescriptive judgments do, in fact, recognise that these judgments are valid only in certain situations and that different linguistic choices are appropriate to different situations (McKeith, 1982). The problem seems to be not lack of awareness, but the absence of a theoretical framework which enables this knowledge to be incorporated systematically into educational practice.

It is not only language testers and teacher trainers who lack an appropriate framework for dealing with a wide range of styles; most academic linguistic work on the subject is limited in one way or another. Thus, for example, the comments of Halliday, McIntosh and Strevens (1964) are not supported by systematic observation. While the analysis of Crystal and Davy (1969) on the other hand *is* firmly based on systematic observation of a range of written and spoken texts, it is largely confined to the public or formal varieties in a community repertoire, such as prayers, sermons, racing commentary or academic conversations. One important reason for general ignorance of the nature of linguistic repertoires may be located in what Labov has aptly described as *the observer's paradox*. This may be stated as follows: in order to observe and study the kind of language used spontaneously in a range of situations, we need good quality recordings. Yet if we try to obtain these using the traditional research instrument of an interview, we define the situational context and so distort the object of our observation. Since an interview is in itself a recognisable speech event, a linguistic observer with a tape-recorder is liable to find his data limited to a single, rather careful style.

This is a dilemma rather similar to that experienced by the teacher or the language tester, who also find themselves in clearly defined situations to which specific, somewhat limited, linguistic choices are appropriate. It is for this reason that we move on now to examine methods which have been developed by linguists to minimise the effects of the observer's paradox. It seems likely that these procedures and the findings emerging from them might usefully be taken into account in devising teaching methods or, as

Carroll (1979) has proposed, in working out language proficiency measures which take account of a wider range of language abilities.

6.5 Observing and analysing linguistic repertoires

The earliest systematic attempts to study variation in an individual's repertoire made use of a linear model where styles were characterised as lying along a continuum which ranged from least formal to most formal (see p. 94 above). Speakers used an increasingly high frequency of standardised pronunciations as they ranged along this continuum. It is clear that although such a unidimensional analysis is of considerable theoretical interest to sociolinguists, it has very sharp limitations. Most of us would recognise, for example, the acts of telling a joke, or of ritual teasing, as two distinct speech events; yet it does not seem meaningful to ask which is the more formal, or whether either is more formal than a narrative or an exchange of gossip.

Labov (1981) has noted that his object in constructing this linear model was to obtain a picture of the linguistic norms of a speech community, not to make a general statement about the range of speech styles in a repertoire. He recognises that a naturalistic study of style would require more than a single dimension.

The style closest to everyday informal speech on Labov's continuum is *casual style* – and that is the variety which is the most difficult to record, because of the effect of the observer's paradox. It is clear that any successful study of the codes in a community repertoire requires extremely carefully planned fieldwork, designed to diminish as far as possible this observer effect to which language is dramatically sensitive. Two studies are cited here as illustrating how the observer's paradox might be partly overcome; that of Labov, Cohen, Robins and Lewis (1968) in Harlem, New York City and that of Milroy and Milroy (1977) in Belfast.

It is useful to summarise the main procedures used by both sets of researchers to diminish the effects of the observer's paradox. First, both made use, in one way or another, of the effect of group dynamics on linguistic style; it is a common experience of fieldworkers that the presence of a group greatly diminishes the effects of observation on language. Second, in both studies, the fieldworkers adopted to some extent the role of participant observers rather than interviewers, retreating where possible to the periphery of the groups. Third, 'insiders' to the group under observation were used in different ways as helpers.

We should note here that all three of these techniques have the effect of reducing the social distance between the field worker and the speaker. The resemblance of the recording situation to a 'test' situation is also considerably reduced. Both studies were successful in eliciting large volumes of spontaneous speech in a range of styles, and some of the detailed findings which bear on the structure of the less formal styles in the repertoire will be discussed below.

It is important always to bear in mind that without careful attention to methods of elicitation, very little information of this kind could have become available for analysis. Thus, the work described here is relevant to any serious discussion of an individual's language abilities, for the reason that it enables us to broaden the data base on which judgments of language ability might be made.

6.5.1   The Harlem Study

The research of Labov and his team in Harlem received government funding largely as a result of official concern at the chronic academic underachievement of black adolescents in America's inner cities, and the tenor of the research report reflects this general concern.

At the time of the research, it had been fashionable in the United States to lay the blame for reading problems and a high dropout rate from school first on the language and then on the cultural environment of black speakers: the claim was that both were in some way deficient. Labov's arguments that the language was deficient only if measured (from a middle-class point of view) against standard English are now well known. Many of his studies of the core grammar of black English ended with the familiar conclusion that as a linguistic system, Black English functioned as well as any other and was *different* rather than *deficient* with respect to standard English. Although the difference–deficit controversy is no longer a live issue in academic circles (an excellent account may be found in J. R. Edwards, 1979), its implications for language teaching and language testing procedures have not, as far as we know, been *systematically* explored or discussed.

With regard to the *use* made of Black English Vernacular in the community (a question now of the communicative competence of its speakers), Labov examines two distinct kinds of speech event – the narrative and the ritual insult. Rather than looking at the ability of a black child to perform in the classroom or in a similar situation of challenge and difficulty set up by outsiders, he examined the capacity of blacks to perform narratives, covering a range of ages from pre-adolescent through to adult. His major point was that the linguistic complexity of the narratives, as measured by the use of various syntactic devices such as subordinate structures, modals and comparatives, increases with age. The result is that older and more skilled narrators are able to use these devices with great dramatic effect and for quite specific purposes (Labov, 1972b:395). It seems to follow from this that oral narrative is quite a specific skill which black speakers learn to use as part of their developing communicative competence; the fact that this skill is less valued than (say) skill in handling a job interview or a test situation is a consequence of the explicitly goal-directed function of these speech events (a social matter), not the greater cognitive skill associated with being a good interviewee as opposed to a good narrator. Thus, the skilful oral narrator has language abilities which, if recognised, can be built upon and expanded. The difficulty appears to be that since the educational system has quite appropriately concentrated on developing the more formal linguistic skills, no systematic framework has emerged for recognising other types of linguistic ability and using *them* systematically as a basis for developing formal skills which may be lacking.

Labov's article finishes somewhat polemically as he compares the narrative ability of black working-class speakers favourably with that of white middle-class speakers. This appears to be seen as the reciprocal of the middle-class speaker's characteristically greater skill in speech events involving public negotiation, control of which is critically bound up with the distribution of power within society (see Barić, 1980 for a fairly abstract discussion of this issue). Control of narrative skills, on the other hand, is not associated with the exercise of power.

The second vernacular speech event discussed by Labov is 'sounding' – a name for the ritual insults exchanged by the boys whom he studied. They take the form of insults, chiefly sexual or scatological in character, directed against a relative of the addressee. The basis structure of the speech event is as follows: 'A sound against B; the audience evaluates; B sounds against A; his sound is evaluated [by the audience]' (Labov, 1972b:327). If B's contribution is an original or well-delivered transformation of A's, B may be said to have won; if not, A may be said to have won. In either case, success is measured by audience response. A may then top B's response with a further transformation, thus producing a sequence like the following, which is based on a tradition of insulting the mother:

1   Your momma's a peanut man
2   Your momma's an iceman
3   Your momma's a fireman
4   Your momma's a truck driver
5   Your father sells crackerjacks
6   Your mother looks like a crackerjack

The last sound in this sequence cannot be topped, combining as it does elements from the penultimate and previous sounds, and the sounding goes off in a completely different direction.

There are various traditional and unflattering attributes with which kin may be accredited and which underlie the structure of sounds such as these. The example given here exploits the attribute of lack of femininity; others may be extreme blackness, ugliness or dog-like characteristics.

Although there is a temptation to dismiss sounding as a childish game involving little in the way of special linguistic or cognitive skills, there are, in fact, quite advanced skills in sounding well. The most important ability seems to be to produce short, decisive closures; also, the insults must be kept ritualised. Labov emphasises that a good sound must emerge clearly as a ritual rather than a personal insult, so that the expression *your family is poor* is not a ritual insult, but a personal one. Since good sounders take great trouble to produce concise, vivid propositions which cannot easily be interpreted as personal insults, they need quick wits. They must be able to process very rapidly short, well-worded sentences.

Labov's analysis of narratives and ritual insults has been considered in some detail here, because it provides rare systematic evidence of the character of speech events of a publicly unrecognised and socially submerged kind. These, in the same way as more public speech events like debating or interviewing, require a developing skill to be mastered before speakers can be said to be fully competent in them. It is important to emphasise this fairly obvious point, while still agreeing that the major task of teachers is to develop skills in the more formal styles – or in Brown's terms, in handling message-oriented utterances. But the problem is that children like those studied by Labov are not usually criticised in terms of limited control of the formal styles of English; despite Labov's work, they are still usually considered to be suffering from some general but unspecified linguistic inadequacy. If we are to move beyond this over-generalised approach to the linguistic problems of non-standard speakers, one necessary preliminary seems to be a discussion of communicative competence, focused on the problem of defining the range of a speaker's existing language abilities. We also need some detailed documentation (such as Labov has provided) of a range of informal styles which gives clear evidence of the presence of advanced language abilities. Otherwise, it is hard to see how the formal linguistic skills which are lacking can be explicitly identified and taught, while *existing* skills are still acknowledged.

We turn now to examine some data from Belfast which gives us a different kind of insight into the communicative competence of non-standard speakers; it suggests the kind of contrast we might expect to find between the characteristic speech style of *interviews* and that of more informal speech events such as narratives or 'sounds'.

6.5.2   The Belfast data

We present here three short transcripts (A, B and C) taken from data collected in Belfast. Extract A is taken from the beginning of an interview (informal in tone, but still an interview) where the fieldworker is questioning a middle-aged working-class man about his life in the community. By way of contrast, neither B nor C can be described as interviews, in the sense that the fieldworker is neither selecting the topics nor controlling the discourse by means of direct elicitation. Transcript B is taken from a very long recording of an interaction between S, a nineteen-year-old boy, and B, his mother. Several of his friends are present, and although they say nothing, their presence is important (see below). The fieldworker, who has been present in the room for some time, says nothing at all during this part of the interaction.

Extract C is also marked by absence of domination by the fieldworker, whose role is confined to giving minimal indications of attention and assent. Present in the room are P, a middle-aged

Clonard woman who has held the floor at this point for an hour with sequences of narratives, all on the topic of the civil disturbances in Belfast. Her teenage daughter, M, also plays a minimal role in the discourse, corroborating and amplifying her mother's version of events.

The structural differences between what might be described as *Interview Style* on the one hand, and two different *Spontaneous Styles* on the other, emerge quite clearly when we examine these three short extracts:

(A)

FW (fieldworker):	/well could you tell me/first of all you say you were born here/ could you tell me where you were born/	(1)
I (informant):	....uh..../Parker Street in East Belfast/.	(2)
FW:	..../a wee bit across the road/and when did you come to live here/	(3)
I:	/here uh/....just about three years ago/....	(4)
FW:	/yeah. and have you ever lived outside East Belfast	(5)
I:	/uh. for a period/....	(6)
FW:	/when/	(7)
I:	..../a couple of year in Ballybeen/. it's actually Ardcairn/ Ballybeen was an extension from that you know/....	(8)

| FW: | /oh yeah/how long for/ | (9) | |
| I: | ..../just a few year/ | (10) | |

(B)

B:	/I got this house 'cos they were pulling the bungalows down/	(1)	Quiet
B:	/ah but they didn't move us from out of there/so they didn't/	(2)	Louder
	we came off our own bat	(3)	
S:	ah we moved ourselves/	(4)	Quiet
S:	squatted/we squatted/	(5)	Very loud
B:	we did not indeed squat/	(6)	Even louder
S:	we did/	(7)	Loud
	we squatted/	(8)	
B:	*when you're* a squatter you've no rent book/	(9)	Loud
	I've a rent book to show anybody/	(10)	
	I've a *rent book*	(11)	
S:	/*ah you're* not a squatter now/	(12)	Loud
	but when you first came here you were a *squatter*	(13)	Loud
B:	/*I've a* rent book from the very *first*/	(14)	Loud
S:	/*When you* first came here you were a squatter/'cos I		

	remember/I had to climb over the yard wall and all/	(15)	Boys laugh
B:	/all right we had to get in that way/	(16)	Quiet
S:	/squat/	(17)	Loud
B:	/we didn't dear/	(18)	Quiet
	/a squatter is some-one that doesn't pay rent/	(19)	Boys laugh
	I've my rent book/	(20)	Quiet
	uh this is about the third or fourth rent book I've got issued to me now/	(21)	

(C)

P:	/and we went down to the corner/	(1)	Laughs
	I says here's me. you're not taking him/		High tessitura
	and the da gets the soldier by the neck/		Loud
	and flung him across the wall/		Final consonant lengthened in 'flung'
FW:	/he's a great big man isn't he/	(2)	
P:	Well he'd this officer by the throat/	(3)	
	and he's choking him/and he's shouting. let him go/let him go		High tessitura
M:	/he was going blue in the face/	(4)	Quiet

P:	/then this other one/y'know John McMahon's mother/she came round she says/I saw him getting kicked she says but I didn't think he was your lad/and the other/the big fat soldier was going to kick him in the head and she says/would you do that on your own son/....and this other young soldier says/. MISSUS I had nothing to do with that/	(5)	
			Quieter
FW:	/Yeah/	(6)	
P:	/so between one and another we got him out of the saracen and we brought him up/the soldiers grabbed HER then/	(7)	
M:	/oh ay by the throat/	(8)	Loud

We can see from these extracts that transcription of conversational speech is not an easy matter; none of them resembles a piece of written prose, and punctuation conventions cannot adequately be used to indicate the systematically patterned voice dynamics characteristic of spoken language (see p. 142 below).

Since these extracts are presented only to suggest the manner in which Interview Style differs from the Spontaneous Styles produced when the fieldworker is not controlling the discourse, transcription has been kept as simple as possible. Clear tone group boundaries are marked with a slash (i.e. the 'chunks' of speech

which characterise spoken language are set off from each other),
pauses are marked with each dot representing a pause of up to one
second in duration; obvious fluctuations in loudness and tessitura
relative to a model voice quality are noted; overlapping utterances
(interruptions) are marked by italics.

Even such a crude transcription, which ignores many clear voice
features, reveals several distinctive characteristics of Interview
Style. First, the two-part structure of the discourse is particularly
evident, with the fieldworker eliciting and the informant replying.
Each move can be coded quote unambiguously as an elicitation or
a reply. Interestingly Sinclair and Coulthard's (1975:6) description
of *classroom* discourse, with the teacher eliciting and the pupil
replying, fits Interview Style well:

A more simple type of spoken discourse, one which has much
more overt structure, where one participant has acknowledged
responsibility for the direction of the discourse, for deciding who
shall speak when and for introducing and ending topics.

Comparison with (B) and (C) further reveals that Interview Style
is characterised by a slow pace with pauses between turns, no interruptions, and little fluctuation in tessitura and loudness. The
discourse structure of extract (A) is repeated many times on the
Belfast tapes, and seems not only to be quite characteristic of interviews in general, but to be rather similar to that of classroom
interaction and (we might add) to that of *test* situations. The
discourse pattern known as the *test cycle* is discussed in Chapter 7.
Meantime we should note the general resemblance of Interview
Style, in terms of its discourse structure, to the styles characteristic
of other speech events where one of the participants has
acknowledged responsibility for controlling the discourse.

A clear two-part structure such as that found in (A) may, of
course, become modified in the course of the interaction with
responses becoming elaborated in various ways as the informant
takes partial control of the discourse. However, all interviews
appear to have the same structure in their initial stages.

Extract (B) is taken from a very long recording of interaction
between S (aged nineteen), four of his friends and his mother, B.
The presence of the four friends is important, although their only
role in the discourse appears to be to laugh loudly as S successfully
teases B about the circumstances of a recent change of residence

(cf. the evaluative role of the audience during a 'sounding' as reported by Labov).

There is in this extract no clear two-part discourse structure, and no overt obligation on either participant to control the discourse. Unlike Interview Style, many conversational moves here, such as for example (2), can be coded simultaneously as *reply* and *elicitation* with no clear boundary between these categories. There is much more fluctuation in tempo and loudness than in (A), with many interruptions indicating an overall faster tempo. Finally, the boundaries of the speech event are marked out by quiet speech, relative to the louder voice used in the main part of the teasing session. In fact, after (21) the conversation moved into a more extended narrative with B dominating the discourse.

Extract (C) is also marked by absence of domination by the fieldworker, whose role is confined to giving minimal indications of attention and assent. Again, there is no clear two-part discourse structure.

This speech event is marked clearly as a narrative in a number of ways. First, there is a dominant participant who has privileges of initiating and ending topics, and who is not liable to be interrupted. A number of clear linguistic features mark her utterances here as performed narrative. First, the so-called historic present alternates with the past tense; this use of the historic present in narratives appears to be commonplace throughout the English-speaking world (see Wolfson, 1976).

Second, direct speech is reported, for dramatic purposes, and introduced by the direct speech markers *here's me* (*him*) and *I* (*she, he*) *says*. These clear genre markings of performed narratives are all present in turn (1). A wide range of what might be described as *channel features* are manipulated by P for dramatic purposes. In (1) and (3) she uses tessitura, loudness and abnormal consonant length in this function. In (5), she uses dramatic pause and fluctuation in loudness to focus full attention on Mrs McMahon's dialogue with the young soldier.

Clearly, there is very much more to be said about structural characteristics of the various spontaneous styles, which are clearly marked off from each other and produced in response to different sets of situational constraints and incentives; an adequate analysis would need to take account of various components of situation such as topic, setting and participants, and other categories suggested by Hymes, as well as the 'internal' characteristics of the conversation. However, a relatively simple comparison of (A), (B) and (C) is sufficient here; the structural simplicity of Interview Style, relative to the complexity of two clearly distinguishable Spontaneous Styles, is quite evident.

What is also evident is that a very much larger *amount* of speech is produced in Spontaneous Styles. If we examine extract (A), we see that the proportion of fieldworker's speech is quite high, and that the interviewee says very little. Again, it seems to be generally true, as Labov has noted, that a larger amount of speech and a wider range of structures are available for analysis in spontaneous styles. The linguistic range of utterance types found in interviews and in those situations which have a close affinity with them, tends to be very limited indeed.

In the following chapters, the implications of these points will be explored, so that we can assess the kind of conclusions which might reasonably be drawn from the data produced during a test situation. Meantime, one conclusion which emerges from both the Belfast and the Harlem studies is that the actual linguistic ability of speakers (in terms of both their command of a range of linguistic structures and of quantity of speech produced) is likely to be quite severely *underrepresented* in interview-like speech events. *Yet it is precisely in situations of this type that generalised judgments about linguistic ability are most often made.*

6.6   Conclusion

In this chapter, we have suggested that a focused exploration of the notion of *communicative competence* is essential if we are to examine critically notions of 'correctness' and 'adequacy' in linguistic usage. In both bilingual and monolingual communities, low status speakers who do not command a 'standard' linguistic repertoire are still often characterised (both popularly and by professional educators) as having poor linguistic ability. However, examination of speech events which have low public prestige – such as oral narrative in black American communities – reveals that considerable ability in linguistic organisation is nevertheless required by the skilled practitioner. Furthermore, comparison of different styles produced by working-class speakers in Belfast suggests that judgments of linguistic ability which are made on the basis of an 'interview-like' situation are likely to make use of impoverished data which are quite unrepresentative of further linguistic abilities which may be revealed when a larger portion of the repertoire is examined.

Judgments of linguistic inadequacy are then frequently based not on any objective or realistic measure of linguistic ability, but on an implicit prescription that an individual should have a particular and limited communicative competence. Thus, for example, the skilled narrator will not be credited with any linguistic skill at all if he cannot reveal it appropriately in the prescribed situation; and despite the well-documented sensitivity of linguistic performance to a number of aspects of situational context, judgments of linguistic inadequacy as made in tests and classrooms usually purport to refer to *total* language ability. Seldom are such judgments presented as relevant only to specific situations.

7
'Planned' and 'unplanned' speech events

In Chapter 6 we suggested that any individual speaker is likely to be competent in a number of speech events which are distinguishable by a range of formal characteristics

Still pursuing the question of what might be meant by an individual's language ability and how such ability might be assessed, we change our perspective on communicative competence to explore the kind of skills needed for controlling the more formal styles in the linguistic repertoire.

Spoken language may be divided broadly (according to function) into the categories of *message-oriented speech* and *listener-oriented speech* (Brown, 1982). A rather similar division of language events into *planned* and *unplanned* discourse has been proposed (Ochs, 1979), and we shall examine the characteristics of these two discourse types here. Since this categorisation cuts across spoken and written channels, we look briefly at some of the organisational devices used to structure spoken and written language (see also Chapter 3 for a more general examination of the different functions of speech and writing). Next, we examine the discourse structure of a characteristically *planned* speech event – the interview.

7.1 Spoken and written language

We have already noted that most people, even those who deal professionally with language, have a very hazy idea of what spoken language – especially informal spoken language – is like. There is a strong general tendency to characterise speech in terms of writing with comments such as 'Doubt has a silent *b*'; 'What does it *say* in the papers?'; 'He drops letters off the ends of words like *huntin'* and *shootin''* (Stubbs, 1980:22). In fact, spoken language is primary and written language a later development in terms both of the individual and the community; but as some kinds of formal speech are organised in a manner similar to written language, the relationship between the two channels is complicated. When the nature of everyday spoken language *is* discussed, it is frequently characterised as lacking in explicitness, ambiguous, incomplete and repetitive. We turn our attention now to this general character-isation.

A transcript of a piece of spontaneous conversation generally looks quite unlike either a piece of written text or the transcript of a piece of language read aloud, such as a radio talk. We have already seen (p. 134) that this is true of the spontaneous speech of low status speakers in Belfast; but it is important to emphasise that the spontaneous speech of educated speakers also is structured in a manner equally different from a piece of written prose. For exam-ple, the following is taken from a conversation between two teachers, discussing over coffee the topic of sex education:

A   it's very awkward/ it's difficult mind you/ with a class of thirty odd/ -occasionally with the second form/ -you get-you know/. well we'll.we'll- have erm- a debate/ –

B   m/

A   what do you want to talk about/ and this is something I usually spend one lesson.arranging what they want to talk about/ and then- tell them to go away and think about it/ and we- have the discussion a later.a later lesson/ and often enough/. round about the second form/ oh/. sex before marriage sir/ or just sex/ instruction/ or should sex be taught in schools/ you know/ (After Crystal, 1981:91)

In addition to *syntactic* differences between spoken and written language of the kind discussed in Chapter 4, other organisational differences are evident here. Much recent work in conversational analysis has shown that the structure of conversation including hesitations, repairs, repetitions and use of 'fillers' (such as *mm, uhuh, well, you know, sort of, I mean*) is highly systematic and serves a range of clear communicative functions (Sacks, Schegloff and Jefferson, 1974; Schegloff, Jefferson and Sacks, 1977; Crystal, 1981). These characteristics are frequently described as 'errors'; yet, since they have a clear function in spoken language, they are errors only if conversation is judged from the normative standpoint of written language (or speech events based upon written language).

In his account of the differences between speech and writing, Stubbs (and see also p. 79 above) has listed a number of formal devices for arranging information and conveying meaning available either to spoken or to written English, but not to both. These are as follows:

> *Speech* (conversation): intonation, pitch, stress, rhythm, speed of utterance, pausing, silences, variation in loudness; other paralinguistic features, including aspiration, laughter, voice quality; timing, including simultaneous speech; co-occurrence with proxemic and kinesic signals; availability of physical context.

> *Writing* (printed material): spacing between words; punctuation, including parentheses; typography, including style of typeface, italicization, underlining, upper and lower case; capitalization to indicate sentence beginnings and proper nouns; inverted commas, for instance to indicate that a term is being used critically (*Chimpanzees' 'language' is*....); graphics, including lines, shapes, borders, diagrams, tables; abbreviations; logograms, for example, &; layout, including paragraphing, spacing, margination, pagination, footnotes, headings and sub-headings; permanence and therefore availability of the co-text. (Stubbs, 1980:117)

Thus, since devices available to *speakers* for organising their linguistic presentation are quite different from those available to *writers*, effective use of the two channels involves quite different skills.

As some speech events may be organised according to the principles appropriate to written language, it is generally quite easy to arrange in conventional written format a text such as a lecture which is read aloud. Sometimes the converse happens, and pieces of writing appear to be organised as if they were spoken – like the following extract which is taken from the written work of a secondary school child in Northern Ireland:

> I really enjoyed myself until when we where racing and on the second last lap and I went over the mound of mud and some of it stuck to the wheels and mudguard and then over the stones and finally the stream but I was so much in to the race and going so

fast that on the bump before the stream I went up and jumped over the stream.

Fairly clearly, there are present here syntactic features characteristic of spoken language, such as a preference for co-ordination rather than subordination (note the absence of relative clauses). It is extremely difficult to see how, without reorganising the syntactic framework entirely, *punctuation* could be used to attain a further level of organisation; yet, the passage makes perfect sense if read aloud, organised into the appropriate *intonational* units. Thus, the difficulty appears not to be a problem of general linguistic capacity, but quite specifically one of handling resources such as literary syntactic constructions, which could then be used in conjunction with punctuation conventions as a means of imposing order on a piece of writing (see Perera, 1984 and in press for a systematic comparison between the syntactic structures characteristic of speech and those characteristic of writing). Unfortunately, there appears to be no simple one-to-one relationship between, for example, intonation and punctuation which might permit an easy transfer between the two channels.

7.2 Planned and unplanned discourse

So far, we have looked at the contrasting formal characteristics of *speech* and *writing*. However, the fact that such speech events as lectures, sermons and speeches depend on written texts in various ways makes it useful to think also in terms of the distinction between *planned* and *unplanned* speech events.

The linguistic skills which are admired in our culture are often associated with speech events which are planned in the sense that they are organised in advance and may even be executed with the aid of notes, memorisation, or reading aloud. Many of the characteristics of conversation noted in the previous section are absent from these more formal events, where the impression is one of careful preplanning, generally on the principle associated with organising written language.

An illuminating direct comparison between the features of planned and unplanned discourse may be found in an article by Ochs (1979). The author's method was to elicit personal narratives, delivered under two separate conditions, by the same speaker. On

the first occasion the speaker (a student) related the narrative orally, without preparation: on the second a narrative of the same event
was written, and turned in as a class assignment.

The following passages are the planned and the unplanned versions of an account by a student of how, while waiting for a train,
he had to catch hold of a woman standing near to prevent himself
from falling from a railway platform. The woman started to fall as
well, but was stopped by a nearby man:

(a) *Planned*
     The train sped nearer as we were both ready to fall off the
     edge. A friend with whom she had been talking, clutched
     her other arm and steadied her as I pulled on the purse's
     shoulder strap moving closer to her arm. My balance was
     finally steadied and it wasn't until after some exchanges of
     looks did I move on with a quick 'Excuse me'.

(b) *Unplanned*
     and it seemed like a long time when it happened but when
     I look back at it it happened just like that ((snaps his
     fingers)) this man-this guy there almost casually looked
     over at 'er and just grabbed her ((laugh)) and looked at me
     like I had the nerve to assault 'er. it was like how dare you
     ((high-pitched)). (After Ochs, 1979:63–4)

While direct comparisons such as these throw into focus the
formal differences between planned and unplanned discourse, one
very serious difficulty with Ochs's approach should be noted;
unplanned *speech* is being compared with planned *writing*. The
planned passage has a distinctly literary flavour; for example, a
'literary' lexical choice such as *sped* seems unlikely in most kinds
of planned *speech*. Nevertheless, the advantages of having a paired
set of data such as (a) and (b) available for comparison outweighs
the disadvantages of Ochs's approach. For although Brown's
analogous distinction between message-oriented and listener-
oriented speech (see p. 119 below) presents fewer theoretical difficulties, no sets of data comparable to Ochs's are provided.

One conclusion drawn by Ochs from a comparison of pairs like
(a) and (b) is that standard modes of syntactic analysis which
employ functional categories such as subject, verb and object as
sentence constituents may not be particularly applicable to
unplanned discourse; however, *planned* discourse can certainly be

analysed in these terms. For example, the general sense of passage (b) suggests that in line 4, the subject of the verb *looked (she)* has been deleted. The preceding direct object is apparently deployed as the deleted subject of the following predication.

Ochs has found that these deletions occur frequently and systematically in unplanned discourse, but in planned discourse they do not occur. Nor are they mentioned in descriptive grammars of English, despite their regular and frequent occurrence. Therefore, it appears that descriptive grammars, our best source of information on the patterns underlying English utterances, reflect the structure of planned rather than unplanned discourse; and of course the vast bulk of anyone's language production comprises *unplanned* discourse.

Similarly, Crystal (1980) has noted that the categories used in syntactic analysis simply do not work well for spontaneous speech (even educated spontaneous speech) which has a regular structure but one quite different from that of formal speech. Givón (1979) has gone further, arguing strongly that modes of thinking about language accepted by professional linguists have always been, and continue to be, adapted to highly planned and standardised speech events which are a small minority of all speech events but are readily amenable to observation. The implication of this comment, discussed in some detail by Givón, is that we lack a true science of language since we are quite ignorant of how to describe, analyse or assess the unplanned discourse which comprises the bulk of all language events.

We might add to these remarks by Ochs, Crystal and Givón that the low social value placed on unplanned discourse allows the apparently considerable structural difference between planned and unplanned discourse to go largely unremarked. Coherent linguistic descriptions of planned discourse are apparently accepted as norms for the language as a whole by those who, for professional purposes, need such descriptions, while unplanned discourse is characterised as containing 'errors' or as 'unstructured' in relation to the norms of planned discourse.

We conclude this section by looking at two further features of unplanned discourse, amongst several specified by Ochs. These features listed below tie in, in an interesting way, with generalisations which have been made by the sociologist Bernstein about working-class language:

1. In relatively unplanned discourse more than in planned

discourse speakers rely on the immediate context to express propositions. (Ochs, 1979:62)

2. In relatively unplanned discourse more than in planned discourse, speakers rely on morpho-syntactic structures acquired in the early stages of language development. Relatively planned discourse makes greater use of morpho-syntactic structures that are relatively late to emerge in language. (Ochs, 1979:68)

Both features are strikingly similar to the characteristics which Bernstein, in his many papers published between 1958 and 1973, has attributed to his *restricted code*. This code has been said to be particularly characteristic of working-class speakers and to arise from culture-specific socialisation patterns.

Although Bernstein's definition of the *restricted* and *elaborated* codes has changed over the period of this work, he has quite consistently described the restricted code as *implicit*, *particularistic* and *context bound*, as opposed to the elaborate code more frequently controlled by higher status speakers which is *explicit*, *universalistic* and *context-free*. Formal (and planned) speech events are in fact characterised by an absence of reliance upon immediate context for their interpretation, and by conjunctions such as *because*, *therefore*, *since* which express explicitly temporal and causal relationships between clauses. It is morpho-syntactic elements of this kind to which Ochs is referring in (2) above. Whether or not Bernstein is right in relating preference for one code rather than the other to culturally different modes of social control (and ultimately to very different underlying symbolic systems) it is likely that codes theory could be reformulated in terms of the variable ability of speakers to control the features which characterise planned discourse. We have already noted that the speech events which require prior organisation are, like Bernstein's elaborated code, associated primarily with speakers who are of relatively high status and have control over society's major resources. Since planned discourse and written language are closely associated with one another, it is likely, as Stubbs (1980) and L. Milroy (1973) have pointed out, that acquisition of the elaborated code is tied up with acquisition of literacy. In a parallel observation, Brown has noted the similarities of her message-oriented speech to Bernstein's elaborated code, and argued 'that this highly structured language is parasitic upon written language and that it is extremely hard to develop it in the absence of control of written language skills'

(Brown, 1982:82). Since Bernstein approaches code theory from the perspective of the non-linguist, and for theoretical sociological rather than linguistic purposes, the parallels between his two codes and Ochs's two discourse types is noteworthy.

An interesting related point is that the organisational principles underlying planned discourse (and writing) in most European languages are in a direct line of descent from the rhetorical principles of classical prose composition (Blatt, 1957). Certainly, some of Ochs's more detailed 'features of planned discourse' have appeared in English only since about the early sixteenth century when an autonomous English prose style was developed, constructed quite explicitly on classical models (see Baugh and Cable, 1978 for a readable and informative history of English). Thus, command of the elaborated code (or the principles of planned discourse) may have more to do with traditional, class-related attitudes to education and literacy (and access to them) than, as Bernstein suggests, with class-related modes of social control. This alternative formulation of class-related differences in language use is supported by recent empirical work in language acquisition (Wells, 1985).

7.3 The discourse structure of interviews

We move on now to examine the structure of a formal type of speech event – the interview – at the level of discourse rather than as we have been doing so far, in terms of organisational characteristics but without reference to communicative context.

The resemblance has already been noted between a structurally simple type of discourse, labelled Interview Style, and the type of discourse which takes place in the classroom between teacher and pupil.

However, a third element of structure often occurs in Interview Style which seems to be particularly common in instructional contexts. Typically, the teacher elicits (E), the pupil responds (R) and the teacher provides evaluative feedback (F) before proceeding to a further elicitation:

T: Those letters have special
    names. Do you know what it
    is? What is the name we give
    to those letters?   (E)

P: Vowels   (R)
T: They're vowels, aren't they?   (F)
T: Do you think you could say
    that sentence without having
    vowels in it?   (E) (Coulthard, 1977:103)

As Coulthard goes on to point out, this three-part discourse pattern (elicitation–response–feedback) is so common in classrooms that absence of feedback is often a sign that the pupil has not provided the answer the teacher wants. Its occurrence in assessment, as well as instructional contexts, is so frequent that it has been aptly labelled *the test cycle* (Wald, 1981:238).

Sometimes feedback is present in minimal form in interviews. Thus, on p. 132 above the interviewer's moves (5) and (9) contain the item *yeah* which seems to function as evaluative feedback. Immediately this is followed by a further question.

A two-part discourse structure, which may optionally include a third part, seems to be characteristic quite generally of a social asymmetrical situation where one (or more) speakers has the responsibility for asking questions (and evaluating replies) and the other(s) for answering them. One of these two formats – that is, either a two-part or a three-part structure – is usually present in a test or assessment situation of any kind, whether it is (for example) a job interview, an interview following a claim for welfare benefits, or a formal language assessment. Although, as Wald (1981:240) points out, the three-part test-cycle is a very salient pattern in test situations, some procedures explicitly require the tester to refrain from providing feedback; an example is the Reynell Developmental Language Scale, on which see p. 159, below.

Neither the two nor the three-part discourse structure typical of these socially asymmetrical situations seems to be at all common in spontaneous conversation. For example, neither type occurs in the two samples of spontaneous speech transcribed in Chapter 6 and both types are very rare in the hundred or so hours of speech tape-recorded in Belfast, being limited mainly to initial interactions between the fieldworker and a single informant. They did not occur when the fieldworker was able to drop the role of interviewer, nor did they occur in interactions between peers, except for a very limited number of exchanges.

In practice, as we might now suspect, the whole notion of 'answering a question' is a very complicated one , and is the subject of an extensive literature. Consider the following data, taken from a stretch of classroom discourse. At this point, the teacher has just played to the class a tape of a man with an unfamiliar accent in order to discuss reactions to accent with the children. The italics are ours:

TEACHER: What kind of person do you think he is?
     Do you – *What are you laughing at?*
PUPIL: Nothing.
TEACHER: Pardon?
PUPIL: Nothing.
TEACHER: You're laughing at nothing, nothing at all?
PUPIL: No.
     It's funny really 'cos they don't think as though they were there they might not like it and it sounds rather a pompous attitude. (Coulthard, 1977:108)

The interrogative *What are you laughing at?* can be interpreted either as a *request* for information or as a *directive* to stop laughing. In the classroom, it is usually the latter, and the pupil has interpreted it in this way. The teacher has to work quite hard to convince the pupil that the sequence is, in fact, a request for information.

The pupil's difficulty is part of a more general point that, depending on situational context, utterances can be interpreted in a wide range of ways. Thus, given certain rights and obligations holding between participants, and certain contextual conditions, a declarative such as *It's dinner time and I'm hungry* can be interpreted as a directive. Under other conditions it may be interpreted as a statement with no directive force (see Stubbs, 1983a for a clear account of the principles of discourse analysis generally). The point is, that unless the context is specified, there is no clear one-to-one relationship between interrogatives and questions or declaratives and statements. Thus, an utterance like *It's dinner time and I'm hungry* which may be analysed syntactically as a declarative sentence may, in context, function as a request for action or for information. For example, a response such as *It'll be ready in twenty minutes* would be perfectly appropriate.

Even allowing for the fact that a given syntactic structure may function in context in various ways, interrogatives seem to be a special problem in that they are associated strongly and rather generally with interactions between persons who are asymmetrical with regard to power or status. The intrinsically threatening and challenging nature of interrogative questions is discussed in detail by Goody (1978) who argues that where interactants stand in a socially asymmetrical relationship to each other, a direct question will nearly always be viewed as a mechanism of social control, or as a command, and seldom as a simple request for information. This explains the teacher's difficulty and the pupil's evasive reply ('nothing') to what he perceives as a 'control' question. It also helps to explain why persons who are being questioned directly in test situations or in interviews (even relatively informal ones) seldom produce a large volume of speech in their replies. The clearest examples in our culture of speech events where questions have this control function are court-room cross-examinations and interrogations.

If we appreciate that direct questions are generally perceived as having a control function where power relationships between interlocutors are asymmetrical, it becomes clear that proficiency tests of any kind which try to elicit a large volume of spontaneous speech by means of interrogatives are almost certainly doomed to failure. Thus we can specify another reason to be cautious about making global judgments of a speaker's language ability on the basis of evidence drawn from test-like situations.

It does not however follow from these observations that direct questions do not occur in spontaneous unplanned speech; they plainly do. But some recent work suggests that they receive an answer only under a sharply limited set of circumstances. Wilson (1981) argues that in conversations between peers, people do not normally answer questions directly if the reason for asking the question is not reasonably clear. Thus, a question such as *What is the time please?* when addressed to a stranger in the street will normally receive a direct answer, as it is generally accepted as self-evident that persons have a number of good reasons for requesting this information. However, a question like *Have you got red underpants on?*, addressed also to a stranger, is unlikely to elicit the information requested. Quite apart from the tabu nature of the subject matter, Wilson argues, such a question would not receive an answer unless a reason for asking it were given such as *I work for an underwear firm, and I'm carrying out a survey.* Wilson suggests that various strategies are used by conversationalists to locate a questioner's intention if the reason for the question is not understood. These involve (amongst others) responding with a request for further information as to the questioner's intention, or answering the question and then requesting further information. Thus, we have the following sequences:

1. (a)   What age is your mother?
   (b)   Why?
2. (a)   Do you feel all right?
   (b)   Yes, sure. Why do you ask?

(Wilson, 1981:67)

Wilson's work taken along with Goody's arguments on the 'control' function of direct questions, suggests very strongly that a chain of question-answer sequences such as those which occur in interviews are not typical of conversations between peers.

Up to this point we have tried to demonstrate that little is known about the formal properties of most speech events whether at the level of phonology, syntax or discourse. Only the most public styles, usually representing planned discourse, have been systematically described. Furthermore direct questioning seems to be characteristic of a socially asymmetrical type of discourse, and so is likely to be perceived as having a control function, or even to be hostile or threatening, where such a social asymmetry exists; it is certainly a very poor means of eliciting information about a person's language ability. Indeed, readers may recall that the linguistic data reported in Chapter 6 (p. 128) which allowed the linguistic ability of non-standard speakers to be examined in terms of a range of speech events, was *not* elicited by means of direct questioning.

Although there is available a large amount of evidence that direct questioning is a poor instrument for eliciting information about general language ability, in schools, clinics and other locations judgments about the linguistic and other abilities of persons unfortunately continue to be made on such a basis. For this reason we look now at the effect on a child's language performance when some of the relevant situational and linguistic variables are manipulated.

7.4 Applying sociolinguistic principles to test situations: an example

A description of the experiment discussed in this section may be found at the beginning of Labov's well-known article 'The Logic of Non-standard English', written in 1969. A reprint is easily available in Giglioli's (1972) collection of papers on sociolinguistic topics to which page references here refer. Although important and influential, the article is somewhat out-dated and should be read with attention to the context in which it was written. Polemical in style and intent, it was designed to counteract the notion prevalent in the United States in the 1960s that the language of disadvantaged black children was inadequate and deficient, and needed to be replaced, for educational purposes, with a more adequate language. Labov's contention was that it was methods of collecting, analysing and interpreting the data which were inadequate; there was nothing at all wrong with the language of low-achieving black children in terms either of its quantity, quality or potential for use in intellectual contexts. The problem, Labov argued, lay partly in the educational system's failure to recognise and build on a child's existing verbal abilities, and partly in the social system which encourages in assessors 'a strong bias against all forms of working-class behaviour, so that middle-class language is seen as superior in every respect – as more abstract, and necessarily somewhat more flexible, detailed and subtle' (p.183). Quoting from Bernstein here, Labov suggests that American educationalists such as Bereiter and Engelmann have, as a consequence of this bias, distorted the views of Bernstein on the differences between working-class and middle-class language behaviour and used them as a justification for intellectually unjustifiable theories and professional practices.

According to one commentator (J. R. Edwards, 1979), Labov was extremely successful in this paper in demolishing the notion of *language deficit* and promoting *language difference* as a more reasonable idea. Certainly, deficit theories are extremely hard to justify intellectually, and it seems likely that they stem ultimately from the deeply entrenched prescriptive ideologies which we have been discussing in this book. It would certainly not be the first time in the history of science that theories and measurement techniques could, with hindsight, be seen to have been developed in order to support intellectually and morally unjustifiable social attitudes (see Gould, 1982 for an excellent historical study of such theories).

Labov's paper is still well worth discussing, despite its age and polemical intent. Few later scholars have been able to comment so illuminatingly on the contrast between the formal language of interviews, and peer-oriented spontaneous speech styles. The part of the paper which chiefly concerns us here is a description of an interview, illustrative of many hundreds carried out in a New York City school. The procedure is that a young black boy enters a room where a friendly white interviewer places an object on the table and asks the child to 'tell me everything you can about this'. This technique results in monosyllabic replies and long periods of silence between the interviewer's questions. The problem is that the results of interviews like this are taken as measures of the verbal capacity of the child although, as Labov notes, his own experience with black children, outside the adult world of home and school, is quite different.

With reference to our discussion in this chapter and Chapter 6 we can make a number of quite specific observations about the validity of viewing the child's performance in such an interview as a representation of his total language ability. First, language is very sensitive to situation, and this is an extremely specialised kind of situation. Second, an *interview* with the classic question/answer format is an extremely unpromising instrument for obtaining very much language at all. Third, outside the interview situation, the *amount* of speech available for analysis increases dramatically; so also does the quality, in the sense that a larger number of different structures is displayed. Finally, it is extremely difficult for the lower status person in a situation of social asymmetry to view questions as anything but tests; Labov suggests that silence is, in fact, a way of defending oneself against criticism in a 'hostile and threatening situation' (p. 185). We have seen that Goody's analysis of questions makes a similar point.

In fact, as Labov shows, the extent to which manipulation of situational and linguistic variables changes the testee's language behaviour is quite dramatic. First, a black researcher was used to carry out an interview with Leon, a 'nonverbal' eight-year-old black boy. The topics (street fighting and television) were selected for their known appeal to eight-year-old boys. But interestingly these changes alone were insufficient to break down the social constraints of the interview situation despite the sympathetic approach of the interviewer. Several further changes were then made, with a view to redefining the speech event more radically. These changes took the form of the following action by the interviewer, who:

1 brought along a supply of potato chips changing the interview into something more in the nature of a party;
2 brought along Leon's best friend, Gregory;

3   reduced the height imbalance (when Clarence got down to the floor....he dropped from 6 ft. 2 in. to 3 ft. 6 in.);
4   introduced taboo words and taboo topics, and proved to Leon's surprise that one can say anything into our microphone without any fear of retaliation. (p. 188)

As a result of these four changes the amount and style of speech elicited became dramatically different; the previously 'non-verbal' eight-year-old now interrupts and competes actively for a chance to speak. Most significantly, Labov's transcription shows that the question/answer format breaks down as the interviewer's role, rather like that of the fieldworker in Belfast (see p. 135 above), becomes one of giving minimal indications of attention and assent.

The crucial change in the total situation appears to be the *reduction of perceived asymmetry* between participants in the speech event. If this is accomplished it becomes possible to define the situation as something other than a test. Consequently, linguistic output is not limited to the evasive and minimal responses which would be predicted in such a situation.

This experiment shows clearly the importance of considering systematically the influence of situation on language as a preliminary to reasonable assessment of language proficiency, and the implications of adopting a more flexible approach to the collection and analysis of data are considerable. For example, an educational or remedial programme would have a better chance of success if it were based on an assessment of a child's *total communicative competence* rather than on a small part of that competence, observed under unfavourable conditions.

7.5   Some wider implications

The points raised in these chapters on the nature of communicative competence and linguistic repertoires are relevant to persons who are concerned with teaching, eliciting or assessing language. What appears to be needed is a more professional and objective approach to language, of the kind which should be adopted in any field of scientific enquiry. The findings and principles of modern linguistics could certainly be incorporated into professional practice to a much greater extent than they are now, and an example of how this might be done will be discussed in detail in the following chapter.

We have expressed the view throughout this book that the strength and social function of prescriptive ideologies militate against an objective and professional approach to language. Individual professionals tend to polarise, or to be seen as polarised, on the issue of how non-standard language should be handled in educational and test situations. As a postscript we may note that entrenched prescriptive attitudes have implications of a very serious kind far beyond educational and test situations. So far, it has been argued that an understanding of the notions of communicative competence and linguistic repertoire reveals that a realistic picture of language ability is unlikely to emerge in a classroom or test situation. However, a recent analysis of a *cross-cultural job interview* suggests that these conclusions might apply to that situation also. It is shown that a mismatch of assumptions between interviewer and interviewee concerning the linguistic behaviour appropriate to the speech event can leave the English interviewer with the impression that the Asian job applicant is professionally incompetent, and the Asian with the impression that he is the victim of racial discrimination.

The problem appears to be partly that the British norms governing the speech event which we might label a *job interview* are assumed rather than explicit. Thus:

> The applicant is expected to show enthusiasm for the *particular* job as a sign of his motivation and commitment. The Asian interviewee, on the other hand, if he uses the criteria which apply in his country of origin, brings a different set of cultural assumptions to the exchange. *For him, the interview is primarily a test, an opportunity to reject him; he therefore counters this by giving yes/no answers without further elaboration wherever possible.* He may even deny knowledge or experience of a particular skill or trade unless he is confident that he could answer any questions on that subject. [Our italics] (Furnborough *et al.* 1982:225).

The italicised comments emphasise the limitations of the interview in this context also as a means of eliciting language; we see again the perception of an interview as a test, and its tendency to elicit monosyllabic replies which in turn stems from the interviewee's awareness of the control functions of questions.

But here, in a situation of considerable importance to the economic well-being of the interviewee, the seriousness of the consequences seems to be compounded. Language is being elicited not to study its structure, but for the sake of the information which it carries. And the assumption that the interviewee will be maximally informative is, as we would now expect, not shared.

Researchers such as Furnborough and his co-authors associated with the Centre for Industrial Language Training have constructed training programmes for industrial personnel (see Gumperz, Jupp and Roberts, 1979), based on analyses of communicative behaviour. The interpretation of communicative competence adopted in these studies of cross-cultural communication is based on the approach of John Gumperz (see, for example, Gumperz, 1982) and is very much broader than the one presented in this book. Gumperz, characteristically, is concerned not only with the constraints of the situation on *linguistic* behaviour, but also with the different uses made by speech communities and individuals of pitch and loudness, gesture, body-space and silence. Above all, he is concerned with the inferences which persons are culturally conditioned to draw from the comments of others.

7.6 Conclusion

We explained in Chapter 6 the related notions of *communicative competence* and *verbal repertoire* emphasising that the repertoires of individuals and communities might differ, and might cut across language boundaries. Judgments about language ability are usually based on a very narrow range of linguistic performance, and are made without much firm knowledge of the nature of spontaneous speech. Furthermore, as we saw in this chapter, most analytic comments about language, including those of many professional linguists, tend to be applicable mainly to 'planned discourse', which has close affinities with written language.

For specifiable sociolinguistic reasons, the interview is likely to be a very poor instrument for eliciting an individual's best linguistic performance, and the implications of this fact are very wide indeed, extending beyond educational and assessment contexts to job interviews. Thus, failure to make a realistic assessment of an individual's language (or of his ability as expressed linguistically) may have far-reaching social consequences. In the concluding chapter, we look in more detail at present language assessment practice, and at how a systematic application of linguistic principles might work.

8

Some practical implications of prescriptivism: the linguistic adequacy of language assessment procedures

8.1 Introduction

Throughout this book, we have considered linguistic prescriptivism from two perspectives. First, we have looked at a number of popular and general notions of correctness in language in relation to known facts about linguistic structure and use, and language history. Second, practical questions have been discussed as they emerged, particularly questions of interest to educators. Generally, we have argued that objective and disinterested discussion of important practical issues connected with 'correctness' (such as the problems of non-standard speakers in the educational system) has been rare, with the result that language teaching and assessment procedures are often less efficient than they might otherwise be.

We now consider one particular practical matter, an area of activity where an objective and informed approach to the facts of language structure and language use would seem to be particularly important; that is the manner in which *language tests* are used to measure, for various purposes, the linguistic abilities of an individual.

In addition to an extensive general literature (mainly within psychology) dealing with the design, scoring and interpretation of tests, there is a somewhat scattered literature produced by linguists which discusses in some detail the *linguistic* adequacy of language tests. It is this second, relatively limited, question which concerns us here; we do not attempt to comment generally or extensively on language testing.

Commentary on the linguistic adequacy of tests appears to be focused on two broad related issues. These are the *linguistic realism* or otherwise of tests – that is, whether they embody in their design an accurate conception of the contemporary language. This matter is discussed in some detail by Crystal, Fletcher and Garman (1976). The second issue concerns the possibility of *cultural-linguistic bias* in test design, and we have already seen that the plaintiffs in the Ann Arbor Black English trial criticised the Wepman Test of Auditory Discrimination for this reason (see p. 114 above).

In the United States generally, a great deal of commentary has dealt with the question of possible bias, apparently in response to recent social legislation concerned with improving the opportunities of ethnic minorities. Language tests are widely used in the United States to measure a child's linguistic ability, and so determine the kind of education most appropriate to him if he has encountered difficulties in the educational system.

In Britain, on the other hand, language testing does not appear to be so widely used in the educational system, and has not become a focus of social and political concern. The British commentary which we will discuss here is less concerned with the question of cultural-linguistic bias than with the linguistic realism of tests (but see Wells, 1984, who suggests that language tests used in the educational system underestimate the ability of working-class children in this country).

8.2 Linguistic critiques of language tests: the question of linguistic realism

One particular British context where tests are very widely used is that of the Speech Therapy Services. Speech therapists routinely use a range of tests (both British and American in origin) to screen their patients for a range of phonological, syntactic and other language disorders, and to assess the nature and relative severity of a patient's impairment. Some norm-referenced language tests (such as the Northwestern Syntax Screening Test or the Illinois Test of Psycholinguistic Ability) are designed to measure the impairment against a developmental norm, while others (such as Schuell's test, which is widely used for adult aphasics – see Schuell, 1973) measure the patient's performance against an adult norm.

Our experience, derived from observation of and discussion with speech therapists from various parts of the British Isles, is that while widespread use is made of standardised tests, individual therapists often view them with some scepticism and supplement them with their own home-made elicitation procedures, in order to gain further insight into the nature and severity of a language disorder. Often, where possible, therapists use and interpret tests with considerable caution and are well aware of many of the problems inherent in their design. For example, in Northern Ireland, many therapists are acutely aware of the difficulties of using a test such as Reynell's Developmental Language Scale (designed to assess production and comprehension over a large but ill-defined area of syntax and semantics) which has been standardised on a South Eastern English population. While the test instructions incorporate strict rules designed to ensure uniformity in administration (see Reynell, 1983), therapists are not provided with a principled way of dealing with problems arising from the comparability or otherwise of different populations. (That such problems do exist is shown by Wiener, Lewnau and Erway (1983). They find, in their comparison of scores achieved by children on a number of standardised tests, that speakers of Black American English differ significantly in their performance from children belonging to the population on whom the test has been standardised.)

Bearing these comments in mind, we look next at the kind of problems which can arise for the language tester as a result of variation in language use, even where the test (unlike Reynell's) attempts to take account of language variation. Such an attempt – made by the authors of the Edinburgh Articulation Test – may be seen as tackling aspects of *both* the issue of linguistic realism (since all real languages are variable), and that of possible cultural bias (since the test allows responses other than those which are coded in Standard English). However, we concentrate in this section principally on the matter of linguistic realism.

The Edinburgh Articulation Test (EAT) is designed to measure a child's phonological development both quantitatively (by means of an age-equivalent score) and qualitatively in order to pick out general phonological patterns from his responses and so establish general remediation guidelines (for details, see Anthony, Bogle, Ingram and McIsaac, 1971). The aspect of the test which concerns us here is the explicit instruction to therapists that they should take into account local dialectal norms in scoring an item as 'correct' or 'incorrect'. This is generally an important issue; as we shall see, one of the conclusions reached by Wald (1982) in Southern California, was that tests in general did not discriminate between vernacular and underdeveloped forms.

The problem for users of EAT is that the instructions are not always easy to implement in a consistent and principled way, even for relatively sophisticated therapists. This is largely because knowledge of vernacular forms is often confined to well-known stereotypical features.

It is fairly clear, for example, that a therapist administering the EAT would score absence of post-vocalic *r* in the item *soldier* as incorrect in Scotland and Ireland but correct in England or Wales. This is because rhoticity is a well-known Scottish and Irish feature. Similarly, speech therapists in the London area are likely to be aware of the rule which variably merges /f/ and /θ/ in London English. Thus, pronunciation like [fʌm] and [fri:] for test items *thumb* and *three* may quite properly be counted as correct in London, but incorrect in Belfast, where they would be underdeveloped rather than vernacular forms. But the problem is that not all vernacular forms are as well-known as this. Thus, in Belfast, there is a vernacular rule which variably deletes [r] in initial clusters, most usually where there is a preceding fricative (e.g. *throw, fruit, three* – see J. Milroy, 1976). An item like *three* would be likely to be affected by the rule, while *string* would not (both appear on the test). Thus, the realisation [θi:] could be a normal Belfast vernacular form while [stɪŋ] probably could not and so would have to count as incorrect.

Our experience has suggested that therapists simply do not have such detailed knowledge as this of vernacular forms. Similarly, while many therapists are aware that there is a vernacular rule in Belfast which results in the variable deletion of [ð] between vowels – as in the EAT item *feather* – many are not aware of the extent to which in normal communities, the rule is applied. (In fact our own findings were that young men delete the consonant in spontaneous speech eighty-nine per cent of the time – about twice as often as women on average (Milroy and Milroy, 1978).) As a result of this uncertainty about the scope of the rule in the speech community, therapists appeared to vary in their scoring of a realisation of *feather* ([fäər] is one example) where the intervocalic consonant was deleted. The issue is further complicated by the fact that generally in children's phonological systems the consonant [ð] is likely to develop late (Cruttenden, 1979). Thus, therapists who have learned this well-known fact about child phonology may be predisposed to judge a pronunciation like [fäər] as under-developed. On the whole, it seems to be the case that where therapists *are* aware of vernacular norms such as /ð/ deletion, they tend, like the public generally, to underestimate the strength of such norms in the community, assuming that they are marginal phenomena confined to a small proportion of a normal individual's casual speech. Systematic investigation of the kind we have described in Chapter 5 often shows that this is not the case. How general examples such as these are in the test, and the quantitative effect of different 'correctness' judgments by therapists have simply not been established. But work on similar problems in syntactic and vocabulary tests has revealed that a very large proportion of test items could be scored as 'wrong' by testers without a reasonable knowledge of dialect variation (see p. 167 below). Since phonology is generally considered to vary dialectally very much more than syntax, we should be cautious of dismissing the examples discussed in this section as insignificant or marginal.

The more general point we are making however is that therapists are faced with a problem implementing the perfectly proper in-struction in the EAT manual, that correctness should be judged in relation to dialectal norms. Quite simply, they vary widely in their knowledge of such norms, and as a result, an identical performance may receive different scores from different therapists. In principle, it ought now to be possible to resolve this particular problem by providing therapists with a handbook outlining the variation in consonant systems and realisations found in English (see Wells, 1982 for a recent account). This should not be a difficult task, as interdialectal variation affecting consonants (and it is mainly consonants with which speech therapists are concerned) is less extensive than inter-dialectal variation affecting vowels.

Problems in the design and administration of tasks which are intended to assess *syntactic* ability seem to be rather more severe than those we have noted in the Edinburgh Articulation Test (which is, phonologically, relatively sophisticated). The prescrip-tive approach inherent in the design of these tests has been noted by Crystal, Fletcher and Garman (1976), who propose an approach to screening, assessment and remediation based on a *comprehen-sive*, *systematic* and *linguistically realistic* comparison between the patient's performance and *both* adult *and* developmental linguistic norms. The patient's language use is described in terms of a profile.

A profile examines language ability by describing relevant features
of an individual's language use with either an adult or a developmental norm providing the comparator, and should give enough
detailed information about language use for the therapist to infer
linguistic guidelines for the design of a remediation procedure.
Unlike a test, a profile does not make use of a set of standardised
questions or tasks in order to elicit a set of responses (Crystal,
1982:2).

One of the difficulties which Crystal, Fletcher and Garman find
with current language tests and procedures – and indeed with the
conception which many therapists have of syntax – is a tendency
to rely on the norms of the written language as characterising
'normal' language and to think of speech as having 'little' or 'no'
or 'debased' grammar (p. 12). We have already seen that this
tendency to characterise speech in terms of writing is a common
approach to linguistic description. Crystal *et al.* note specifically
that therapists are frequently unhappy about admitting items such
as *don't, won't, can't, isn't* into the remedial context, often feeling
that they should present 'good' models to their patients. The fact
is, however, that contracted negative auxiliaries of this kind are
extremely common in spoken English. Lee and Canter (1971:326)
are quoted as saying of the equally common contractions *gonna,
wonna* and *gotta* that 'children should not be penalised for this
articulatory error'. While it is clear that therapists are often reflecting general public anxiety – for these attitudes to correctness are
extremely common ones in the Western world – it is important in
remedial contexts to distinguish sharply at all times between
pathological forms on the one hand and colloquial or vernacular on
the other. As Crystal and his colleagues demonstrate, a failure
to adopt a linguistically realistic approach frequently leads to
unrealistic remediation strategies:

> An example of artificiality in sentence structure may be found in
> the tendency to make sentences longer by symmetrical expansion
> of the elements of structure, e.g. Noun + Verb (NV) becomes
> NNV then NNVV, then NNNVV, then NNNVVV and so on,
> which rapidly produces absurd structures. Conn (1971) gets into
> difficulties over this, for instance. One of his sentences develops
> into *Jack and Jill are washing Jim and Jane* to which a cor-
> responding question stimulus is proposed: *Whom and whom are
> Jim and Jane washing?* [sic] (Crystal, Fletcher and Garman,
> 1976:12)

A different problem is that if spoken norms are ignored (or simply not explicitly identified), normal spoken features tend, as a result, to be stigmatised. An example quoted by Crystal *et al.* is the issue of *and* as a clause-linking device (which is particularly common developmentally amongst normal children at around the age of three).

Another example of a spoken norm which is often stigmatised is conversational ellipsis, which occurs particularly frequently in response utterances. Thus, the answer part of the following sequence is quite likely to be branded as 'not proper grammar', the desired (but actually somewhat abnormal) response being 'the squirrel is in the tree':

A: Where is the squirrel?
B: In the tree

In fact, this is a common and normal response type to a question such as A. Elliptical responses of this kind differ from incomplete or ill-formed sentences in that they are derivable from the structure of the previous utterance and so take the structure of that utterance for granted. Thus, the ellipted utterance B involves the deletion of the subject and verb which are present in the previous utterance. As Crystal *et al.* point out (p.95) it is important for a therapist to know how far a patient can take previous sentence structure for granted in this way; certainly, a capacity to produce well-formed elliptical sentences should not be judged as ungrammatical. Labov (1972d) has also noted the widespread tendency of language tests to stigmatise normal ellipsis.

A further consequence of confusing spoken with written norms is that bizarre syntax of a kind which seldom occurs in everyday speech is frequently found in language comprehension tests. For example, one of the more difficult linguistic stimuli used by Nelson and McCroskey (1978), modelled on a similar stimulus item from the Northwestern Syntax Screening Test, is 'The daddy showed the baby the doggie'. The testee is required to associate the stimulus with one of four possible picture representations. Crystal *et al.* also note the existence of characteristic 'test' syntax: an example is frequent use of the simple present tense as in 'the boy goes'. In everyday language, this construction is relatively unusual except where habitual reference is intended; 'the boy is going' is much more likely. In a similar vein, Fillmore (1981:251) has commented on American standardised reading tests:

> The testing industry, we have come to realise, has created a new genre for English written language, a genre whose characteristics are determined by very unnatural requirements of lexical choice, grammatical structuring and synonym alterations.

One major problem then appears to be that test design (which follows psychological, not linguistic academic practice) is predicated on an unrealistic conception of the fully developed form of the language; therapists have generally been given little guidance in this matter. A further problem, stemming from this same lack of appreciation of the nature of the spoken norm, is a tendency to focus selectively in tests on limited, easily identifiable bits of the syntactic system. Thus, for example, the Grammatic Closure Subtest of ITPA concentrates on morphology (see also p. 167 below) and does not attempt an assessment of less easily identifiable, but equally (if not more) important aspects of syntactic ability which are capable of discriminating normal from language-impaired children extremely successfully.

An example is the ability to produce an expanded verb phrase within a clause containing three elements of structure. The following sequence, which demonstrates this point, is taken from the transcribed speech of a twelve-year-old girl in a Belfast special school, for whom a syntactic profile was later constructed:

T(herapist):   What's John doing?
P(atient):   He's writing.
T(herapist):   Is he writing a letter?
P(atient):   No / He writing the homework.

The interesting point here is that P was able to realise the clausal element V (Verb) with the verb phrase *is writing* (Auxiliary + Verb) in her first utterance where the clause was of the relatively simple SV (Subject + Verb) type. But as soon as a further clausal element was added, as in her second utterance, giving an SVO (Subject + Verb + Object) type clause, her verb-phrase structure collapsed, with the loss of the auxiliary *is*.

This particular pattern of weakness where an expansion at clause level tends to result in a collapse at phrase level is very common in children with syntactic disability (see Crystal, Fletcher and Garman, 1976:114 for a discussion of this 'trade-off' tendency). Equally common is a specific weakness in the *verb* phrase of the kind demonstrated here. Since the auxiliary in English is functionally very important, the consequences of this weakness for the girl's ability to communicate efficiently are very far-reaching. Particularly, the order of the auxiliary in relation to the other elements of structure has to be manipulated in a complicated way by speakers to construct well-formed questions, negatives and passives (see Quirk, Greenbaum, Leech and Svartvik, 1972). One of the consequences of the girl's weakness in the verb phrase was, in fact, that she could not easily manipulate her syntactic resources to ask questions, negate, or produce passives.

We are emphasising here the weakness of language tests which allow only for 'right' or 'wrong' responses, focusing selectively and uncritically on portions of the grammar which happen to be prominent and easily quantifiable. They do not usually attempt to measure these more subtle but important aspects of language ability. Yet any linguistically realistic assessment needs to take into account the hierarchical structure of language and so to look in some detail at the inter-relationship between phrase and clause structure. In fact, the syntactic profile designed by Crystal and his colleagues analyses systematically, at the levels of the clause, the phrase and the word, various aspects of the patient's syntax. This analysis is used as an aid to assessing language abilities and working out remediation strategies.

Relying extensively on the work of these linguists, we have tried in this section to outline the problems which loom large when language tests are constructed without due regard to the facts of normal language structure and use, and conclude that over-simplified notions of the nature of normal language result in rather impoverished assessment and remediation instruments. Such an over-simplification of language structure is quite characteristic of most doctrines of correctness, and it is clearly these popular correctness doctrines, rather than careful linguistic analysis, which underlie the design of many language tests currently used to assess the mother tongue language abilities of English speakers.

8.3 Linguistic critiques of language tests: the question of cultural linguistic bias

In the United States, much more than in Britain, language testing appears to have become a controversial public issue. This is apparently because the results of language tests are used very widely in the educational system to help determine the kind of education most appropriate to the child encountering problems at school. It frequently happens that the children identified by these tests as having language problems are members of minority ethnic groups, or rural dialect speakers. Clearly, this difference between Britain and the United States in the *application* of language testing procedures gives rise to different practical outcomes. While inadequate tests in British speech therapy clinics may result in rather inefficient (and time-consuming) assessment and remediation procedures, inadequate tests in the American context are likely to result in loss of educational opportunity. This is a much more serious social and political matter, and accounts for the concern which gave rise to the issue of language testing being raised in (for example) the Michigan Black English trial (see p. 114 above).

We have already seen that the use in Michigan of the Wepman Auditory Discrimination Test as an assessment instrument resulted in a diagnosis of the plaintiffs' children as having language and auditory perception problems. Since this test required the children to discriminate between minimal pairs like *reef/wreath*, *pin/pen*, the argument was put forward by the defence that it was biased against Black English and Southern dialect speakers who often pronounce these pairs the same. It was argued that as the test required the children to make phonemic distinctions not present in their dialect, it was likely to underestimate the development of their auditory perceptual skills. Examination of the Wepman scores as entered in the children's school records showed that this had actually happened.

Although the difficulty encountered by these children was indeed one of auditory discrimination, their low scores should not have been taken as showing that they had perceptual and auditory *problems*. The fact is, that if a speaker whose dialect does not contain the /f/ /θ/ contrast is asked to discriminate between a minimal pair which depends on that contrast, he is liable to filter out the auditory information which he needs in order to perceive the contrast, because it is linguistically irrelevant. Thus, he is less likely to perceive the contrast than is a standard speaker, for whom it is linguistically functional.

Similar problems are encountered by speakers learning a foreign language with a system of contrasts different from the native language, a simple example being the difficulty perceived by many

English-speaking learners of French in distinguishing between front and back high rounded vowels (cf. *rue* v. *roue*). The English vowel system has no comparable distinction in this phonetic area.

General discussion of problems associated with tests such as the Wepman and the Templin Darley Test of Articulation (which assess aspects of phonological development) are provided by Wolfram (1974) and Taylor (1977, 1982). Wolfram points out that the social effect of these tests should not be underestimated; they are widely used to assess reading-readiness in kindergarten and pre-school children, where frequently their results have been used as a basis for establishing extensive language intervention and compensatory education programmes. (A useful critique of such programmes may be found in J. R. Edwards, 1979.)

Developmental tests are widely used in the United States to measure grammatical ability and vocabulary development also. Careful analysis of some of these has suggested that they too are fairly sharply biased against non-standard speakers. Wolfram (and see also Wolfram and Christian, 1980) looks in some detail at the Illinois Test of Psycholinguistic Ability (ITPA), which contains a battery of sub-tests designed to measure grammatical development. ITPA is an assessment instrument well known to speech therapists in Britain also; we have already noted (p. 164 above) that the Grammatic Closure Sub-test has been criticised by British linguists because of the unprincipled selectivity of the items tested, and Wolfram criticises it for other reasons which are outlined below.

The procedure in the Grammatical Closure Sub-test is for the child to supply a missing word in a sentence when the tester points to a stimulus picture. For example, he may show a picture of two beds to the child, point to one, and say 'here is a bed'. Next, he points to both and says 'here are two ——'.

The purpose of this item is to assess whether the child can produce plurals correctly. All the items in the sub-test require the child to supply a morphological element of some kind, and they must be in standard English to be considered a correct response. Thus, for example, the child who responds with *hisself* for *himself*, *mans* or *man* for *men* or *hanged up* for *hung up*, is scored as incorrect. Out of a total of 33 items in the sub-test, Wolfram calculates that 27 may legitimately have different dialect forms. It is, of course, not to be expected that a given speaker will use non-standard forms for all 27 items; but if non-standard responses are given to even a fraction of these, the effect will be to depress systematically the scores of non-standard speakers. (See Wiener, Lewnau and Erway, 1983 for a systematic investigation of this difficulty.)

Similar comments may be made about one very widely used test of vocabulary development – the Peabody Picture Vocabulary Test. This test (which is familiar in Britain also) has, in fact, been subjected to considerable criticism for some years, usually on the grounds that many items are potentially culture-specific. Roberts (1970) has commented that 13 of the first 50 items (26%) are potentially culture-specific to speakers of non-standard English. Wolfram gives the item *spectacles* as an example of such culture specificity, remarking that many young children may be unfamiliar with that item, but quite familiar with the synonyms *glasses* or *eyeglasses*.

These comments by linguistic analysts are particularly relevant in view of the fact that in the United States, non-standard speaking groups score very much lower on language tests than do standard speaking groups. As Wolfram and Christian (1980:170) note, most research suggests that this difference stems from a bias in test materials rather than from any important difference in ability. This seems to be true regardless of whether the difference in ability is held to be associated with intellectual superiority or with environmental factors. If indeed language tests are to function in the way they are intended to do – as a useful tool for educators – there appears to be some need to develop more effective instruments for identifying the population with genuine language problems.

The problem at the moment, identified by Wolfram and others (see, for example, Wald, 1981; Taylor, 1982) is that the results of tests like these are often used to support arguments that non-standard speaking testees lack language ability in some unspecified way. Scores are thus used to lend apparent objectivity to judgments based on prescriptive ideologies of the kind which we have been considering in this book. Yet it is clear that well established but, in this context, unjustifiable notions of correctness are inherent in the design of tests, as indicated (for example) by the ITPA requirement that responses should be in standard English.

It is, then, perfectly possible to specify in some detail the test items in which bias might be detected. However, many writers consider that there is in many tests a bias against non-standard speakers which is more serious but much less tangible than is implied by the discussion so far.

Both Wolfram and Taylor point out that standardised testing

(not necessarily language testing) is an important means of assessment in the United States, inside the school system and elsewhere. For example, both the Civil Service and the Armed Forces assess the aptitude of applicants by means of standardised tests. Plainly, language is used in all tests to give directions and encode information content of items.

This widespread use of standardised testing as a mode of assessment is predicated on the assumption that standardised tests are objective; this assumption in turn does not appear to take into account differences in communicative competence between different groups of speakers. The assumption of objectivity is questionable, argue Wolfram and Taylor, because of differences in the general orientation of different groups towards the task of testing. A review of similar objections by others (not necessarily linguists) may be found in J. R. Edwards (1979:50–74).

It is generally pointed out by these critics that a test situation is a highly specialised event, with its specific rules for participants (cf. the comments on p. 120 above concerning the communicative competence of different social groups). It should not automatically be assumed to be neutral with regard to the social group of the testee. As a number of investigators have remarked (Wald, 1981; French and McClure, 1981), the three-part discourse structure already referred to as the *test cycle* is very common in test situations (see p. 145 above for an example). One important aspect of the initial question in the test cycle is that it is *not a genuine request for information*; that is, the child knows that the tester knows the answer to the question. Moreover, the child often has to give obvious information accessible already to the tester, in identifying a picture, an activity or an object. As Labov has pointed out, children often respond in conditions like this with silence, which then may be taken as an inability to encode a linguistic answer to the question. This objection reflects a more general problem associated with language testing, formulated in the following way by Corder (1973):

If our test is to do its job properly, it must not incidentally or accidentally measure anything else [other than language ability], for example the learner's intelligence, his knowledge of the world or his system of beliefs. In other words, the test must be *valid*. (p. 356)

Corder then goes on to define *validity* of a test (after Pilliner, 1968:30) as 'the extent to which it does what it is intended to do'.

In fact, in order to do well in a test, the child has to grasp that the test cycle is a specific communicative event, and that the initial question functions as a request for a display of knowledge. The child who grasps this and responds with an appropriate display of knowledge is likely to be more successful than the child who responds with silence even though both children may control the syntactic and semantic components of the linguistic system equally well. Thus, Corder's and Pilliner's conditions for a valid test seem to be violated if these possible differences in communicative competence are not taken into account in the test design. It is often suggested (see, for example, Wells 1985:333; Wolfram, 1974 and Taylor, 1977) that middle-class socialisation patterns encourage this kind of display of knowledge, and that test situations may, therefore, be viewed as having, at a rather abstract and hard-to-pin-down level, a built-in bias in favour of middle-class culture which is not explicitly intended or acknowledged. Thus, they are not as neutral as test-designers, and those who make use of tests, assume. As Taylor points out:

> Linguistic and cultural differences in the very activity called "testing" can be a source of bias. These factors alone may have considerable impact on test performance. For example, a basic assumption of standardised testing is that it is perfectly appropriate for the testee to (a) be willing to provide obvious information – e.g. *How many eyes do you have?* – and (b) give a performance for a total stranger – the examiner. These basic social assumptions may be in direct conflict with interactional rules for individuals in some cultures. That is, some children may fail to respond to items on a test for reasons that are unrelated to the items themselves, but are related to the task expected. (Taylor, 1977:260)

The implication of these criticisms seems to be that language tests of the kind discussed here are rather poor measures of language ability, but good measures of the testee's understanding of the assumptions underlying language tests. Again, as Corder points out, accomplishing the effective elimination of non-linguistic knowledge is a general problem in devising tests (p.360). Moreover, the differences in testees' understandings of the tasks involved seem to be related to the differences in communicative competence associated with different groups, middle-class speakers often being better able to handle public and formal speech events, of which tests are an example.

Following the general findings outlined in Chapter 6 of this book, that both quality (in the sense of range of linguistic structures used) and quantity of speech is greater if it is spontaneous rather than elicited in a test interview, an extensive piece of research has been carried out in Southern California designed to develop points such as those raised by Taylor and to discover as accurately as possible the effect of situation and topic on language behaviour. This work is fully reported in Wald (1981); we conclude this chapter with a discussion of its major findings.

Wald's work is motivated by a concern for the level of bias in tests (such as those we have discussed in this chapter) which dismiss as worthless language proficiencies deriving from a child's cultural background. One example discussed by Wald is the Bilingual Syntax Measure (BSM), used also for monolingual speakers. BSM gives points for inflections which are regularly absent from the speech of many black monolinguals (e.g. third person singular *-s* and the possessive marker *'s* (p. 28)). Wald's concern is that the results of biased tests of this kind are interpreted by prescriptively-minded educators as showing that low-scoring testees lack proficiency in *any* variety of the tested language rather than the standard variety which the test requires (Wald n.d.:27-8). Thus here, as elsewhere, the problem springs from general ignorance of the nature of 'real' language (see also Rivera, ed., 1983 for a number of papers on the same theme). In a series of articles Wald discusses ways of relating test items more closely to the kind of language abilities needed for education. The general background to the research is the mismatch noted between the naturalistically observed language abilities of low status bilingual and monolingual children in various contexts, and the language proficiency measures assigned by language tests to these same children. In view of the sensitivity of language to topic and situation, Wald notes the difficulty of arriving at a valid assessment of language ability by studying language recorded in a single, rather specialised situation (see Chapter 6 above).

One major empirical study of the language of 10–12-year-old Spanish-English bilingual children in Southern California was carried out specifically as a consequence of a concern with the current practice in the education system of 'categorising students as limited or fluent speakers of English in order to determine their eligibility for services and treatments intended to enhance their opportunites for academic achievements' (1981:1). Wald distinguishes sharply between *language proficiency* as measured by current test instruments, and *language ability*, 'the actual knowledge a speaker has of a language which is made use of in a variety of situations' (1981:2).

Given the fact that language proficiency measures intended to indicate *educational potential* tend to elicit only a tiny proportion of the linguistic structures of which a child is capable, language ability would seem to be the more important concept. Ideally, a language ability assessment instrument should pinpoint specific areas of difficulty and so suggest guidelines for remedial action (cf. the *syntactic profile* discussed on p. 162 above).

Wald's procedure for investigating language ability in a realistic way was to collect language samples in three situations:

1 A *group interview*, where an adult attempts to encourage conversation amongst peers (cf. the methods of Labov, discussed on p. 153 above).

2 A *peer conference*, where the children were left alone with a school-like task for about ten minutes – they were to construct a story to match comic-strip pictures.

3 A *test interview*, where a standardised test was administered.

The similarities and differences between the language behaviour shown in Session Three and the other Sessions formed the basis of Wald's comparison between language ability and language proficiency; his detailed findings, which can be referred to only briefly here, are of some practical importance.

First, a similar pattern of *morphological* development emerges in all three situations. This, of course, does not hold true if the morphological elements measured in the test are non-standard and stigmatised; in that case development tends to be underestimated by the test (see p. 167 above for examples).

Second, *syntax* cannot be adequately sampled in test situations, and information about specific syntactic constructions (such as relative clauses) emerges only in the group interview and the peer conference. The reason for this is largely that extended stretches of speech emerge only occasionally in tests but relatively frequently in narratives. This point would seem to be an important one, as a capacity to handle (for example) relativisation is essential for control of the written language (cf. the example of a child's writing on p. 142 above). Thus, it is likely that the teacher would benefit from accurate knowledge of a child's syntactic ability as a basis for teaching writing skills. One suggestion made by Wald, in fact, is that many so-called language problems could appropriately be reformulated as *literacy* problems, and writing materials matched to developmental stages (1982:20).

One further important point is that formal test procedures cannot discriminate between non-standard forms on the one hand, and under-developed forms on the other, while the distinction emerges clearly if the language of a *group* of children, as opposed to the language of individuals, is examined (cf. also the criticisms by Crystal *et al.* discussed on p. 162 above).

Finally, an important methodological point is that even a ten-minute corpus of spontaneous speech, if skilfully elicited, can yield concrete information about quite specific syntactic strengths and weaknesses. Thus, the argument against many language testing procedures is not only that social bias and prescriptive assumptions are inherent in the design, but also that they are unnecessarily inefficient instruments for measuring language ability. Views similar to Wald's, which stress the importance of analysing language samples collected in naturalistic situations, have, in fact, been expressed also by psychologists who traditionally favour carefully standardised test procedures. For example, Carroll has noted that 'some of the more important language abilities can be established only through studies of language performances in realistic, non-testing situations' (1979:22).

More recently, the authors of a book which explores methods of assessing children's language in natural contexts have expressed similar views somewhat more strongly:

We predict that [the] pragmatics approach will not be just another addition to our evaluation techniques, but that it will shake the very foundations of how we have been approaching children with language problems. Our notion that we can examine children's language by presenting them with controlled stimuli, such as sentences to imitate or formal tests, will come into question. Our idea that language in the clinic is the same thing as language outside the clinic will be suspect. Our hope that we can measures a child's language ability in one context in a two-hour diagnostic session will be demolished as results from the research in pragmatics become known to us. (Lund and Duchan, 1983:6)

8.4   Concluding remarks

One general conclusion which we might draw from this comment- ary on current language assessment techniques is that there is an urgent need to develop a more accurate definition of what con- stitutes a 'language problem'. This is clearly an issue of importance to educators as well as to speech therapists.

No-one can benefit from a situation where literacy problems, developmental problems, and normal but non-standard language ability are confused. One of the consequences of the correctness doctrines which colour our approach to language assessment and teaching is that it is hard to analyse objectively exactly what is wrong with a child who, for whatever reason, has an inadequate control of the standard language. The assumption sometimes made is that an analytic approach to language problems involves 'teaching no grammar' or abandoning standards of correctness (see Honey, 1983 for a recent example of this assumption). However, if we want to design realistic English teaching programmes which succeed in teaching non-standard speakers to use standard English, or to pinpoint more accurately the precise nature of a language problem, we must develop more systematic analytic procedures. And these procedures must take account of the sensitive relation- ship between language performance and situational factors.

Coda

In this book we have explored the historical and cultural background to notions of 'correctness' in language; analysed types of linguistic 'complaint'; offered an appraisal of prescriptive ideologies in the context of contemporary linguistic realities (or the best approximation we can find to these realities), and attempted to show that prescriptivism itself can be seen as having a social function in promoting the 'idea' of a standard. For a standard language remains as necessary as ever in a complex, large scale society such as ours, and needs to be available as a resource to all English speakers

We hope, therefore, that our arguments will not be interpreted as an attack on standard English or on well-informed standards of language teaching and assessment. On the contrary, this book is, amongst other things, a plea for realism and knowledge. There is a depressing general ignorance of the nature of language and the complexity of linguistic issues in society, and linguistic matters have ramifications that are even wider than the practical issues in language testing and assessment that we have chiefly discussed. One of the authors has, for example, had the unhappy experience of reviewing legal evidence that led to a conviction, but which was based chiefly on naive interpretations of unsubstantiated allegations about the defendant's speech (J. Milroy, 1984b). In public life, much of our so called knowledge of linguistic matters is still in the realm of folklore.

To return to the aim of making the standard language available as a resource to all – we have tried to show that the fundamentally narrow approach to language that is still current even amongst professionals directly concerned with language is ill-fitted to achieve this aim. The language abilities of non-standard speakers still continue to be defined in a way which understates them; the notion of communicative competence, with its emphasis upon the sensitivity of language performance to situation of use, is crucial here. The invention and widespread use of the tape-recorder has enabled us to acquire much more accurate knowledge of current realities of language use than was once possible, and yet, as we have tried to show, current public approaches to matters of language teaching and assessment are informed by a theory of language use which has altered very little since Jonathan Swift's time.

But social realities have changed a great deal since the eighteenth century. We now have a majority of non-standard speakers in the school population. We also have in Britain a multilingual and multi-cultural population whose needs for access to the standard language have to be met by a policy worked out in full recognition of those needs, and of their own community language repertoires. A simple demand for cultural and linguistic assimilation is not adequate.

Recently, John Edwards has commented on the difficulties of handling problems associated with social disadvantage, of which he counts language as one of the most important, and certainly the most visible (Edwards, 1981:43).

He remarks (p.42) 'difficulties whose very existence depends upon social standards and social comparisons are among the most intractable. They prove . . . singularly resistant to *rational explanation and objective identification*' (our emphasis).

We hope we have shown that the language problems of non-standard speakers are overwhelmingly dependent on 'social standards and social comparisons' of a very complex and historically deep-rooted kind. Their resistance to rational explanation and objective identification is precisely the reason for the wide scope of this study of language standardisation and prescription. And the absence of 'explanation' and 'identification' has in fact been largely responsible for the quite conspicuous absence of linguistic realism in English language teaching and assessment instruments, even those, like standardised language tests, which are seen as 'objective' and 'scientific'. The same absence of 'explanation and identification' of language problems is also in large part responsible for the low level at which they are publicly discussed. It has in fact been our depressing experience while completing this book to follow a public debate of this level over a period of several months. We hope that the book will contribute in a constructive way to a realistic analysis of the language problems of non-standard speakers.

Bibliography

Aitchison, J. (1978), *Linguistics*, Sevenoaks, Kent, Hodder & Stoughton (Teach Yourself Books).

Aitchison, J. (1981), *Language Change: Progress or Decay?*, London, Fontana.

Amis, K. (1980), 'Getting it Wrong', in Michaels and Ricks (eds), 24–33.

Anthony, A., Bogle, D., Ingram, T. T. S. and McIsaac, M. W. (1971), *The Edinburgh Articulation Test*, Edinburgh and London, Livingstone.

Barić, L. F. (1980), 'Dominant Language and Cultural Participation', MS, University of Salford.

Baugh, A. C. and Cable, T. (1978), *History of the English Language*, 3rd edn., London, Routledge & Kegan Paul.

Bell, A. (1982), 'Broadcast News as a Language Standard', MS, University of Reading.

Bernstein, B. (ed.) (1971, 1972, 1973, 1975), *Class, Codes and Control*, vols 1,2,3, London, Routledge & Kegan Paul.

Bickerton, D. (1975), *Dynamics of a Creole System*, Cambridge, Cambridge University Press.

Blatt, F. (1957), 'Latin Influence on European Syntax', *Travaux du Cercle Linguistique de Copenhague*, XI, 33–69.

Blom, J.-P and Gumperz, J. (1972), 'Social Meaning in Linguistic Structures: Code Switching in Norway', in J. Gumperz and D. Hymes (eds), *Directions in Sociolinguistics*, New York, Holt, Rinehart & Winston.

Bloomfield, L. (1933), *Language*, New York, Holt, Rinehart & Winston.

Boissevain, J. (1974), *Friends of Friends: Networks, Manipulators and Coalitions*, London, Blackwell.

Bolinger, D. (1980), *Language: The Loaded Weapon*, London, Longman.

Bolton, W. F. (ed.) (1966), *The English Language: Essays by English and American Men of Letters 1490–1839*, Cambridge, Cambridge University Press.

Bolton, W. F. and Crystal, D. (eds) (1969), *The English Language, Volume 2: Essays by Linguists and Men of Letters 1858–1964*, Cambridge, Cambridge University Press.

Boyd, J. and Boyd, Z. (1980), 'Shall and Will', in Michaels and Ricks (eds), 43–53.

Brown, G. (1977), *Listening to Spoken English*, London, Longman.

Brown, G. (1982), 'The Spoken Language', in Carter (ed.), 75–87.

Carroll, J. B. (1979), 'Psychometric Approaches to the Study of Language Abilities', in Fillmore, Kempler and Wang (eds), 13–31.

Carter, R. (ed.) (1982), *Linguistics and the Teacher*, London, Routledge & Kegan Paul.

Caxton, W. (1490), 'Prologue' to *Eneydos*, reprinted in Bolton, W. F. (ed.), 1–4.

Chambers, J. K. and Trudgill, P. J. (1980), *Dialectology*, Cambridge, Cambridge University Press.

Cheshire, J. (1982a), *Variation in an English Dialect*, Cambridge, Cambridge University Press.

Cheshire, J. (1982b), 'Dialect Features and Linguistic Conflict in Schools', *Educational Review*, 34.1, 53–67.

Chomsky, N. (1965), *Aspects of the Theory of Syntax*, Cambridge, Mass., MIT Press.

Corder, S. P. (1973), *Introducing Applied Linguistics*, Harmondsworth, Penguin.

Coulthard, M. (1977), *An Introduction to Discourse Analysis*, London, Longmans.

Cruttenden, A. (1979), *Language in Infancy and Childhood*, Manchester, Manchester University Press.

Crystal, D. (1980), 'Neglected Grammatical Factors in Conversational English', in Greenbaum, Leech and Svartik (eds), 153–66.

Crystal, D. (1981), *Directions in Applied Linguistics*, New York, Academic Press.

Crystal, D. (1982), *Profiling Linguistic Disability*, London, Arnold.

Crystal, D. (1983), Review of J. Honey's *The Language Trap*, *BAAL Newsletter*, 18, 42–50.

Crystal, D. and Davy, D. (1969), *Investigating English Style*, London, Longman.

Crystal, D., Fletcher, P. and Garman, M. (1976), *the Grammatical Analysis of Language Disability*, London, Arnold.

De Camp, D. (1971), 'Towards a Generative Analysis of a Post-Creole Continuum', in D. Hymes (ed.), *Pidginization and Creolization of Languages*, Cambridge, Cambridge University Press.

Denison, N. (1972), 'Some Observations on Language Variety and Plurilingualism', in Pride and Holmes (eds), 65–77.

Dorian, N. C. (1981), *Language Death: The Life Cycle of a Scottish Gaelic Dialect*, Philadelphia, University of Pennsylvania Press.

Edwards, J. R. (1979), *Language and Disadvantage*, London, Arnold.

Edwards, V. K. (1979), *The West Indian Language Issue in British Schools: Challenges and Responses*, London, Routledge & Kegan Paul.

Edwards, V. K. (1981), 'Research Priorities in the Sociolinguistic Description of Black British English', from *Language and Ethnicity*, Mimeo, University of London Institute of Education.

Fillmore, C. J. (1979), 'On Fluency', in Fillmore, Kempler and Wang (eds), 85–101.

Fillmore, C. J. (1981), 'Ideal Readers and Real Readers', in D. Tannen (ed.), *Georgetown University Round Table*, Washington D.C., Georgetown University Press, 248–70.

Fillmore, C. J., Kempler, D. and Wang, S.-Y. (eds) (1979), *Individual Differences in Language Ability and Language Behaviour*, New York, Academic Press.

Fischer, J. L. (1958), 'Social Influences on the Choice of a Linguistic Variant', *Word*, 14, 47–56.

Fowler, H. W. (1926), *Modern English Usage*, revised by Sir Ernest Gowers, London, Oxford University Press (1965).

French, P. and MacClure, M. (eds) (1981), *Adult-Child Conversation*, London, Croom Helm.

Fries, C. C. (1957), *The Structure of English*, London, Longman.

Furnborough, P., Jupp, T., Munns, R. and Roberts, C. (1982), 'Language Disadvantage and Discrimination: Breaking the Cycle of Majority Group Perception', *Journal of Multilingual and Multicultural Development*, 3, 3, 247–66.

Gannon, P. (1982), 'Responding to Children's Writing', in Carter (ed.), 88–100.

Giglioli, P. P. (ed.) (1972), *Language and Social Context*, Harmondsworth, Penguin.

Giles, H., Bourhis, R., Trudgill, P. and Lewis, A. (1974), 'The Imposed Norm Hypothesis: A Validation', *Quarterly Journal of Speech*, 60, 405–10.

Giles, H., Bourhis, R. and Davies, A. (1975), 'Prestige Styles: The Imposed Norm and Inherent Value Hypothesis', in McCormack and Wurm (eds).

Giles, H. and St Clair, R. (eds) (1979), *Language and Social Psychology*, Oxford, Blackwell.

Gimson, A. C. (1980), *An Introduction to the Pronunciation of English*, 3rd edn, London, Arnold.

Givón, T. (1979), *On Understanding Grammar*, New York, Academic Press.

Goody, E. N. (ed.) (1978), *Questions and Politeness*, Cambridge, Cambridge University Press.

Gould, S. J. (1982), *The Mismeasure of Man*, London, Norton.

Gowers, Sir Ernest (1954), *The Complete Plain Words*, London, HMSO.

Greenbaum, S., Leech, G. and Svartvik, J. (eds) (1980), *Studies in English Linguistics for Randolph Quirk*, London, Longman.

Gumperz, J. J., Jupp, T. C. and Roberts, C. (1979), *Crosstalk: A Study of Cross-Cultural Communication*, Southall, National Centre for Industrial Language Training.

Gumperz, J. J. (1982), *Discourse Strategies*, Cambridge, Cambridge University Press.

Haas, W. (1982), 'On the Normative Character of Language', in Haas, W. (ed.), 1–36.

Haas, W. (ed.) (1982), *Standard Languages: Spoken and Written*, Manchester, Manchester University Press.

Hall, R. A., Jr. (1950), *Leave Your Language Alone*, Ithaca, N.Y., Cornell University Press.

Halliday, M. A. K., McIntosh, A. and Strevens, P. (1964), *The Linguistic Sciences and Language Teaching*, London, Longman.

Harris, J. (1982), 'The Underlying Non-identity of English Dialects: A Look at the Hiberno-English Verb-phrase', *Belfast Working Papers in Language and Linguistics*, 6, 1–36.

Harris, J. (1984), 'Syntactic Variation and Dialect Divergence', *JL*, 20(2), 303–327.

Haugen, E. (1972), 'Dialect, Language, Nation', in Pride and Holmes (eds), 97–111.

Hewitt, R. (1982), 'White Adolescent Creole Users and the Politics of Friendship', *Journal of Multilingual and Multicultural Development*, 3, 3, 217–32.

Honey, J. (1983), *The Language Trap: Race, Class and the 'Standard English' Issue in British Schools*, Kenton, Middlesex, National Council for Educational Standards.

Hudson, R. A. (1980), *Sociolinguistics*, Cambridge, Cambridge University Press.

Hudson, R. A. (1983), Review of J. Honey's *The Language Trap*, *BAAL Newsletter*, 18, 50–4.

Hurford, J. and Heasley, B. (1983), *Semantics: a Course-book*, Cambridge, Cambridge University Press.

Hymes, D. (1967), 'Models of the Interaction of Language and Social Settings', *Journal of Social Issues*, 23(2), 8–28.

Johnson, S. (1755), 'Preface' to *A Dictionary of the English Language*, reprinted in Bolton, W. F. (ed.), 129–56.

Jones, D. (1955), *An English Pronouncing Dictionary*, London, Dent.

Klein, W. and Dittmar, N. (1979), *Developing Grammars*, Berlin, Springer.

Labov, W. (1966), *The Social Stratification of English in New York City*, Washington D.C., Center for Applied Linguistics.

Labov, W. (1972a), *Sociolinguistic Patterns*, Philadelphia, Pennsylvania University Press.

Labov, W. (1972b), *Language in the Inner City*, Philadelphia, Pennsylvania University Press.

Labov, W. (1972c), 'Where Do Grammars Stop?', in R. W. Shuy (ed.), *Sociolinguistics: Current Trends and Prospects*, Washington, D.C., Georgetown University Press.

Labov, W. (1972d), 'The Logic of Non-Standard English', in Giglioli (ed.), 283–307.

Labov, W. (ed.) (1980), *Locating Language in Time and Space*, New York, Academic Press.

Labov, W. (1981), 'Field Methods Used by the Research Project on Linguistic Change and Variation', *Sociolinguistic Working Paper*, No.1, Austin, Texas, South Western Educational Development Laboratory.

Labov, W. (1982), 'Objectivity and Commitment in Linguistic Science, The Case of the Black English Trial in Ann Arbor', *Lang. Soc.*, 11, 165–201.

Labov, W., Cohen, P., Robins, C. and Lewis, J. (1968), *A Study of the Non-Standard English of Negro and Puerto-Rican Speakers in New York City*, Report on Co-operative Research Project 3288, New York, Columbia University.

Lass, R. (1980), *On Explaining Language Change*, Cambridge, Cambridge University Press.

Lavandera, B. R. (1978), 'The Variable Components in Bilingual Performance', in J. Alatis (ed.), *International Dimensions of Bilingual Education*, Washington, D.C., Georgetown University Press, 391–409.

Lee, L. and Canter, S. M. (1971), 'Developmental Sentence Scoring: A Clinical Procedure for Estimating Syntactic Development in Children's Spontaneous Speech', *Journal of Speech and Hearing Disorders*, 36, 315–40.

Leith, D. (1983), *A Social History of English*, London, Routledge & Kegan Paul.

Leitner, G. (1982), 'The Consolidation of "Educated Southern English" as a Model in the Early 20th Century', *International Review of Applied Linguistics*, 2, 91–108.

Linguistic Minorities Project (1985), *The Other Languages of England*, London, Routledge & Kegan Paul.

Luck, G. (1975), *A Guide to Practical Speech Training*, Colchester, Vineyard Press.

Lund, N. J. and Duchan, J. E. (1982), *Assessing Children's Language in Naturalistic Contexts*, Englewood Cliffs, Prentice-Hall.

Lynn, R. W. (1972), 'Problems of Motivation of Learning English', *Language*, Journal of the Singapore Linguistic Society, 1, 113–16.

MacAllister, A. H. (1963), *A Year's Course in Speech Training*, 9th edn., London, University of London Press.

Macaulay, R. K. S. (1977), *Language, Social Class and Education*, Edinburgh, Edinburgh University Press.

McCormack, W. and Wurm, S. (eds) (1975), *Language in Many Ways*, The Hague, Mouton.

McKeith, J. (1982), 'A Study of Attitudes to Language Variants Amongst the Staff of a College of Education', Unpublished M.A. Thesis, New University of Ulster.

Metcalfe, J. E. (1975), *The Right Way to Improve your English*, revised edition, Kingswood, Surrey, Elliot Right Way Books.

Michaels, L. and Ricks, C. (1980), *The State of the Language*, Berkeley, Los Angeles and London, University of California Press.

Milroy, J. (1976), 'Length and Height Variations in the Vowels of Belfast Vernacular', *Belfast Working Papers in Language and Linguistics*, 1.3.

Milroy, J. (1977), *The Language of Gerard Manley Hopkins*, London, André Deutsch.

182 *Bibliography*

Milroy, J. (1978), 'Stability and Change in Non-Standard English in Belfast', *Bulletin of the Northern Ireland Speech and Language Forum* 2, 72–82.
Milroy, J. (1981), *Regional Accents of English: Belfast*, Belfast, Blackstaff.
Milroy, J. (1982), 'Probing Under the Tip of the Iceberg: Phonological Normalisation and the Shape of Speech Communities', in Romaine, S. (ed.), *Sociolinguistic Variation in Speech Communities*, London, Edward Arnold.
Milroy, J. (1983), 'On the Sociolinguistic History of /h/ Dropping in English', in M. Davenport, E. Hansen and M. F. Nielson (eds), *Current Topics in English Historical Linguistics*, Odense, Odense University Press, 37–53.
Milroy, J. (1984a), 'The History of English in the British Isles' in P. Trudgill, (ed.), *Language in the British Isles*, Cambridge, Cambridge University Press.
Milroy, J. (1984b), 'Sociolinguistic Methodology and the Identification of Speakers' Voices in Legal Proceedings', in P. Trudgill (ed.), *Applied Sociolinguistics*, London, Academic Press.
Milroy, J. (1984c), 'Present-day Evidence for Historical Changes', in *Proceedings of the First International Conference in English Historical Linguistics* (Durham, 1979), Sheffield, University of Sheffield.
Milroy, J. and Harris, J. (1980), 'When is a Merger not a Merger? The MEAT/MATE Problem in a Present-day English Vernacular', *English World-Wide*, 1, 199–210.
Milroy, J. and Milroy, L. (1978), 'Belfast: Change and Variation in an Urban Vernacular', in Trudgill (ed.).
Milroy, J. and Milroy, L. (1985), 'Linguistic Change, Social Network and Speaker Innovation', *Journal of Linguistics*, 21, 339–84.
Milroy, L. (1973), 'Codes Theory and Language Standardisation', Mimeo, Ulster Polytechnic.
Milroy, L. (1980), *Language and Social Networks*, Oxford, Blackwell.
Milroy, L. (1984), 'Communication in Context: Successful Communication and Communicative Breakdown', in P. Trudgill (ed.), *Applied Sociolinguistics*, London, Academic Press.
Milroy, L. and Milroy, J. (1977), 'Speech and Context in an Urban Setting', *Belfast Working Papers in Language and Linguistics*, 2, 1–85.
Mühlhäusler, P. (1979), 'Sociolects in New Guinea Pidgin', in S. A. Würm (ed.), *New Guinea and Adjacent Areas: A Sociolinguistic Laboratory*, The Hague: Mouton.
Mühlhäusler, P. (1982), 'Language and Communicational Efficiency: The Case of Tok Pisin', *Language and Communication*, 2.2, 105–21.
Müller, M. (1861), *Lectures on the Science of Language*, vol. 1.
Nelson, N. W. and McRoskey, R. L. (1978), 'Comprehension of Standard English at Varied Speaking Rates by Children Whose Major Dialect is Black English', *Journal of Speech and Hearing Disorders*, 11, 37–50.
Ochs, E. (1979), 'Planned and Unplanned Discourse', in T. Givón, (ed.), *Syntax and Semantics 12: Discourse and Syntax*, New York, Academic Press.

O'Kane, D. (1977), 'Overt and Covert Prestige in Belfast Vernacular Speakers: The Results of Self-Report Tests', *Belfast Working Papers in Language and Linguistics*, 2, 54–77.

Oliphant, T. K. (1873), *The Sources of Standard English*, London, Macmillan.

Orwell, G. (1944), 'Propaganda and Demotic Speech', reprinted in *George Orwell*, London, Secker and Warburg / Octopus (1980), 636–40.

Orwell, G. (1946), 'Politics and the English Language', reprinted in Bolton and Crystal (eds), 217–28, also in *George Orwell*, London, Secker & Warburg/Octopus (1980), 735–44.

Orwell, G. (1949), *Nineteen Eighty-Four*, London, Secker & Warburg.

Palmer, F. R. (1965), *A Linguistic Study of the English Verb*, London, Longman.

Perera, K. (1984), *Children's Writing and Reading*, Oxford, Blackwell.

Perera, K. (1986), 'Language Acquisition and Writing', in Fletcher and Garman (eds), *Language Acquisition*, 2nd edn, Cambridge: Cambridge University Press, 484–518.

Petyt, K. M. (1977), *Dialect and Accent in the Industrial West Riding*, Ph.D. Thesis, University of Reading.

Phaire, T. (1545), *The Boke of Chyldren*, edited by A. V. Neale and H. R. E. Wallis, Edinburgh, Livingstone (1955).

Pilliner, A. (1968), 'Subjective and Objective Testing', in A. Davies (ed.), *Language Testing Symposium*, Oxford, Oxford University Press.

Platt, J. T. (1977), 'The Subvarieties of Singapore English: Their Sociolectal and Functional Status', in W. Crewe (ed.), *The English Language in Singapore*, Singapore, Eastern Universities Press.

Platt, J. T. and Weber, H. (1980), *English in Singapore and Malaysia*, London, Oxford University Press.

Pride, J. B. and Holmes, J. (eds) (1972), *Sociolinguistics*, Harmondsworth, Penguin.

Quirk, R. (1968), *The Use of English*, 2nd edn., London, Longman.

Quirk, R. (1972), *Report on Speech Therapy Services*, London, HMSO.

Quirk, R., Greenbaum, S., Leech, G. and Svartvik, J. (1972), *A Grammar of Contemporary English*, London, Longman.

Radford, A. (1981), *Transformational Syntax*, Cambridge, Cambridge University Press.

Rae, J. (1982), 'The Decline and Fall of English Grammar', *Observer*, 7 February 1982, p.41.

Reynell, J. (1983), *Manual for the Reynell Developmental Language Scales*, Revised edn., Windsor, NFER.

Rivera, C. (ed.) (1983), *An Ethnographic/Sociolinguistic Approach to Language Proficiency Assessment*, Clevedon, Multilingual Matters.

Roberts, E. (1970), 'An Evaluation of Standardised Tests as Tools for the Measurement of Language Development', in *Language Research Report No. 1*, Cambridge, Language Research Foundation.

Robinson, I. (1973), *The Survival of English*, Cambridge, Cambridge University Press.

184 *Bibliography*

Rogers, E. M. and Shoemaker, F. F. (1971), *Communication of Innovations*, 2nd edn., New York, Free Press.

Romaine, S. and Reid, E. (1976), 'Glottal Sloppiness? A Sociolinguistic View of Urban Speech in Scotland', in *Teaching English*, 9, 3, Edinburgh, C.I.T.E.

Ryan, E. B. (1979), 'Why do Low-prestige Language Varieties Persist?' in Giles and St Clair (eds), 145–57.

Sacks, H., Schegloff, E. and Jefferson, G. (1974), 'A Simplest Systematics for the Organisation of Turn-Taking for Conversation', *Language*, 50, 696–735.

Sankoff, G. (1972), 'Language Use in Multilingual Societies: Some Alternative Approaches', in Pride and Holmes (eds), 33–51.

Sankoff, G. (1980), *The Social Life of Languages*, Philadelphia, University of Pennsylvania Press.

Samuels, M. L. (1972), *Linguistic Evolution*, Cambridge, Cambridge University Press.

de Saussure, F. (1915), *Cours de Linguistique Générale*, translated as *A Course in General Linguistics*, London, Duckworth, 1983.

Saville-Troike, M. (ed.) (1977), *Linguistics and Anthropology*, Washington, D.C., Georgetown University Press.

Schegloff, E. A., Jefferson, G. and Sacks, H. (1977), 'The Preference for Self-Correction in the Organisation of Repair in Conversation', *Language*, 53, 2, 361–82.

Schuell, H. (1973), *Differential Diagnosis of Aphasia with the Minnesota Test*, revised edition, London, Oxford University Press.

Scragg, D. G. (1975), *A History of English Spelling*, Manchester, Manchester University Press.

Simon, J. (1980), 'The Corruption of English', in Michaels and Ricks (eds), 35–42.

Sinclair, J. (1982), 'Linguistics and the Teacher', in Carter (ed.), 16–30.

Sinclair, J. M. and Coulthard, M. (1975), *Towards an Analysis of Discourse*, London, Oxford University Press.

Sledd, J. (1962), 'The Lexicographer's Uneasy Chair', reprinted in Bolton and Crystal (eds), 284–93.

Stubbs, M. (1980), *Language and Literacy: The Sociolinguistics of Reading and Writing*, London, Routledge & Kegan Paul.

Stubbs, M. (1983a), *Discourse Analysis*, Oxford, Blackwell.

Stubbs, M. (1983b), *Language, Schools and Classrooms*, 2nd edn., London, Methuen.

Stubbs, M. and Hillier, H. (1983), *Readings on Language, Schools and Classrooms*, London, Methuen.

Sutcliffe, D. (1982), *British Black English*, Oxford, Blackwell.

Swift, J. (1712), 'A Proposal for Correcting, Improving and Ascertaining the English Tongue', reprinted in Bolton (ed.), 107–23.

Taylor, O. (1977), 'The Sociolinguistic Dimension in Standardized Testing', in Saville-Troike (ed.), 257–66.

Taylor, O. (1982), 'Sociolinguistics and Communication Disorders', in N. Lass *et al.* (eds), *Speech, Language and Hearing*, Philadelphia, Saunders.

Todd, L. (1974), *Pidgins and Creoles*, London, Routledge & Kegan Paul.

Tongue, R. K. (1974), *The English of Singapore and Malaysia*, Singapore, Eastern Universities Press.

Townsend, H. E. R. and Brittan, E. M. (1972), *Organisation in Multiracial Schools*, Windsor, National Foundation for Educational Research.

Traugott, E. C. (1972), *The History of English Syntax*, New York, Holt, Rinehart and Winston.

Trench, R. C. (1851, 1888), *On the Study of Words*, London, Kegan Paul (20th edn., 1888).

Trudgill, P. (1974), *The Social Differentiation of English in Norwich*, Cambridge, Cambridge University Press.

Trudgill, P. (1975), *Accent, Dialect and the School*, London, Arnold.

Trudgill, P. (ed.) (1978), *Sociolinguistic Patterns in British English*, London, Arnold.

Trudgill, P. (1983), *Sociolinguistics*, 2nd edn., Harmondsworth, Penguin.

Trudgill, P. and Hannah, J. (1982), *International English*, London, Edward Arnold.

Wald, B. (n.d.), *Report on the Study of Limited Language Proficiency*, mimeo, California, National Center for Bilingual Research.

Wald, B. (1981), 'Topic and Situation as Factors in Language Performance', *NCBR Working Paper*, California, National Center for Bilingual Research.

Wald, B. (1982), 'Situational Effects on the Language Behaviour of Late Primary School Preadolescent Spanish–English Bilinguals: Consequences for Hypothesis Generation', mimeo, California, National Center for Bilingual Research.

Wells, G. (1985), *Language Development in the Pre-school Years*, Cambridge, Cambridge University Press.

Wells, J. C. (1982), *Accents of English*, 3 vols., Cambridge, Cambridge University Press.

Wells, J. C. and Colson, G. (1975), *Practical Phonetics*, London, Pitman.

Whorf, B. L. (1941), 'The Relation of Habitual Thought and Behavior to Language', reprinted in Whorf (1956), 134–59.

Whorf, B. L. (1956), *Language, Thought and Reality: Selected Writings of Benjamin Lee Whorf*, J. B. Carroll (ed.), Cambridge, Mass.: MIT Press.

Wiener, F. D., Lewnau, L. E. and Erway, E. (1983), 'Measuring Language Competency in Speakers of Black American English', *Journal of Speech and Hearing Disorders*, 48, 76–84.

Wilson, J. (1981), 'Come on Now, Answer the Question: An Analysis of Constraints on Answers', *Belfast Working Papers in Language and Linguistics*, 5, 93–121.

Winters, Y. (1966), 'Gerard Manley Hopkins', reprinted in G. H. Hartman (ed.), *Hopkins: A Collection of Critical Essays*, Englewood Cliffs, Prentice-Hall, 37–56.

Wolfram, W. (1974), 'Levels of Sociolinguistic Bias in Testing', mimeo, Washington, D.C., Center for Applied Linguistics.

Wolfram, W. and Christian, D. (1980), 'On the Application of Sociolinguistic Information: Test Evaluation and Dialect Differences in Appalachia', in T. Shopen and J. M. Williams (eds), *Standards and Dialects in English*, Cambridge, Mass., Winthrop, 177–209.

Wolfson, N. (1976), 'Speech Events and Natural Speech: Some Implications for Sociolinguistic Methodology', *Language in Society*, 5, 189–209.

Wurm, S. A. (ed.) (1979), *New Guinea and Adjacent Areas: A Sociolinguistic Laboratory*, The Hague, Mouton.

Wurm, S. A. and Mühläusler, P. (1979), 'Attitudes Towards New Guinea Pidgin and English', in Würm (ed.), 243–62.

Wyld, H. C. (1927), *A Short History of English*, 3rd edn., London, John Murray.

Wyld, H. C. (1936), *A History of Modern Colloquial English*, Oxford, Blackwell.

Index